From Peasant to Entrepreneur

From Peasant to Entrepreneur

*The Survival of the
Family Economy in Italy*

ANNA CENTO BULL AND PAUL CORNER

BERG

Oxford / Providence

First published in 1993 by
Berg Publishers Limited
Editorial offices:
221 Waterman Street, Providence, RI 02906, USA
150 Cowley Road, Oxford, OX4 1JJ, UK

© Anna Cento Bull and Paul Corner 1993

Library of Congress Cataloging-in-Publication Data

Cento Bull, Anna, 1951–
From Peasant to entrepreneur: Survival of the family economy in
Italy/Anna Cento Bull and
Paul Corner.p. cm.
Includes index.
ISBN 0-85496-309-X
1. Italy—Industries, Rural. 2. Peasantry — Italy.
I. Corner, Paul. II. Title.
HC305, C377 1993
305.5'633'0945–dc20   92-25571
                                CIP

British Library Cataloguing in Publication Data

A CIP catalogue record for this book is available from the British
Library.

ISBN 0-85496-309-X

Printed in the United States by E. B. Edwards Brothers, Ann Arbor, MI.

Contents

List of Tables

List of Figures

Abbreviations

ACS	Archivio Centrale dello Stato
DGPS	Direzione Generale Pubblica Sicurezza
AGR	Affari Generali e Riservati
b.	busta
f.	fascicolo
sf.	sottofascicolo
ISTAT	Istituto Centrale di Statistica
MAIC	Ministero Agricoltura Industria Commercio
INEA	Istituto Nazionale Economia Agraria
PCI	Partito comunista italiano
DC	Democrazia cristiana
UPE	Ufficio provinciale economia

Acknowledgements

This study has its somewhat distant origin in the E.S.R.C.–
funded research project 'Industrialisation, Social Change, and
Political Behaviour in Northern Italy 1880–1948' which was
drawn up and directed by Paul Corner (then at the University of
Reading) and John Stuart MacDonald of the University of
London. Both would like to take this opportunity to thank the
E.S.R.C. for its generous support which provided for travel and
research assistance in Italy. Naturally, responsibility for the
present volume rests entirely with Paul Corner and Anna Cento
Bull. For her part, Dr. Bull would like to acknowledge the help
given by the European Commission in financing the survey of
small textile businesses which is mentioned in Chapter 5.

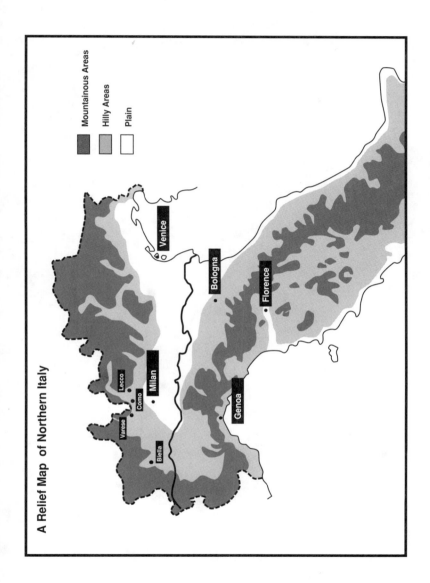

A Relief Map of Northern Italy

Mountainous Areas

Hilly Areas

Plain

Venice

Bologna

Florence

Lecco

Como

Milan

Varese

Biella

Genoa

1
Introduction

Anyone looking through the Table of Contents of this volume might be forgiven for thinking that this is a book about the silk industry in Como during the course of the last hundred and fifty years. In fact it is not – or not precisely that. Histories of the silk industry in the Comasco and the Brianza already abound and it would be pointless to try to add to them in the same terms. Rather, what follows is an attempt to tackle certain broader themes relating to the various phases of Italian industrialisation and to the social and economic forces which helped to form that process. The silk industry, and the Como and Brianza region above Milan, have been selected therefore as an industry and a region which exemplify certain aspects of a specifically Italian process of industrialisation.

The broader themes – those that go beyond the silk industry and the particular region – have to do with arguments which have become familiar in recent years in connection with certain aspects of the economic development of Italy in the 1970s and 1980s. These concern the growth of the so-called 'third Italy' – distinct from the 'first' Italy of the industrial triangle and the 'second' Italy of the underdeveloped South.[1] It is a 'third Italy' made up of previously backward and rural zones of northern and central Italy – zones which had remained largely untouched by earlier industrialisation. These areas have experienced rapid development around the mushrooming of small, family firms – a phenomenon which has led to conjecture about the role played by the rurally-based family, sometimes former sharecroppers but always newcomers to business initiative. The phenomenon itself has been viewed with satisfaction and not a little surprise, in as far as the growth, the success and, in particular, the capacity for survival of small, decentralised, firms has been seen as something new and unexpected, and – as we shall see – has served to upset more than one theory of industrial development.[2]

This book argues that certain of the features of recent development, commonly associated with the affirmation of the

Third Italy, can, in fact, be found elsewhere in Italy and in an earlier period. Through the example of the silk industry and the Comasco, we suggest that many of the factors which have favoured the growth of small businesses are not as new as they might seem, and that, on closer examination, regions of recent boom and areas which saw an earlier phase of industrialisation possess many common characteristics.

Central to this argument is the process of transition from an agricultural to an industrial economy – a transition which has occurred at different times and with varying speeds in the many diverse regions of Italy, and which is by no means completed today. As in all processes of industrialisation, the main protagonist of this transition has been the family, forced to adjust to changes which have threatened the relative stability of centuries. Here, the focus of our attention is the *way* in which some peasant families adjusted to transition. We suggest that the particular relationship which developed between an agricultural population and diffused rural industry determined a *social form* of production – the peasant-worker family – which has persisted over the decades and displays very specific characteristics. The silk industry, which flourished between 1840 and 1930 in rural areas above Milan, offers an opportunity to illustrate this theory; but it is to be stressed that it is not so much the industry itself which is the subject of study as the social form which rural industry produced.

The Lombard silk industry has, of course, for long been recognised as a powerful source of capital accumulation during the first phase of Italian industrialisation. An enormously valuable product, silk cost very little to produce, and consequently yielded very high profits for landowners and silk merchants. And for almost the entire period of liberal Italy, silk constituted around a third of the value of Italian exports. These 'financial' aspects of silk are well known, and have been the objects of a great deal of attention.[3] Much less attention has been dedicated to the history of the peasant families employed by silk, and it is this aspect – the development of the rural workforce – which is the central theme of this study. Silk – whatever else it did for the Italian economy – also helped to produce a very special kind of workforce. In part this was a result of the unique character of silk production, which required the peasant family to work on the land, to cultivate the mulberry leaves, to raise the silk worms at home, and then to work in the factory – to throw and spin the silk thread. The workforce was highly specialised in some senses; but its essential characteristic was that it remained involved in agriculture, as a rural workforce (most peasants were sharecroppers), while at the same time being dependent on introits from the part-time, non-agricultural labour of peasant women and children. This was a mix of activity (so-called 'pluriactivity') which would continue in many areas of the Alto Milanese even when silk production itself had virtually disappeared – the peasant families then turning their attentions to other forms of non-agricultural activity *in order to be able to survive on the land*; indeed, it was at this point that the peasant-worker family, far from disappearing, began increasingly to impose itself on the regional economy, providing the workforce and often the entrepreneurship which lay behind the expansion of a multitude of new small businesses. As a social form, therefore, the peasant-worker family was created by its contact with silk, but was not ultimately linked to that particular activity.

What is interesting in historical terms is that the formation of this workforce does not correspond to the classic model for the creation of an industrial working class, which usually sees workers forced from the land by agricultural modernisation or else induced to leave by the attractions of higher wages in urban industries. Silk created a very different social humus, a different structure of production, and different attitudes to enterprise – all of which nonetheless played an important part in the development of the Italian economy.

Attention to the role of peasant-worker families represents, therefore, a slightly different approach to the question of the formation of the working class from that which has been usual in Italy. The way in which labour moved away from agriculture in order to work in industry has been the subject of research for many years – particularly within the field of studies dealing with the origins of the working class; yet, for obvious reasons of political orientation among historians, the formation of the *urban* working class has been the main focus of attention – something which has tended to limit research to northern Italy (the industrial triangle in the main) and to a particular epoch (generally that preceding the First World War).[4] The interweaving of peasant and industrial activity within the same family – the formation of a worker-peasant, or peasant-worker (depending on where the economic emphasis lay within the family) class – which is a specific characteristic of Italian industrialisation has been to some extent underestimated until now. And here perhaps the models of more heavily industrialised countries such as Britain and Germany have been responsible for suggesting a pattern which conforms only to certain, very limited, areas of Italy. It may be more fruitful – at least for many areas (Alto Milanese, Venetia, certain parts of Emilia, the Marches and Tuscany) to consider an alternative model based on the gradual interweaving of agricultural and industrial employment among workers – a combination which does not always result in the separation of labour from the land. Such a workforce obviously existed in several areas of Italy until very recently; *indeed, it is probable that, for a longer period than is often recognised, production in manufacturing was realised more by workers who were not working class, in the conventional sense of the urbanised industrial worker, than by those who were.*[5] It may prove interesting to try to project this model into the whole process of the formation of Italian industry and the development of the Italian industrial structure. This is a point to which we shall return in our conclusions.

The persistence in Italy of a peasant class – albeit with many variants – beyond what is generally considered to be 'normal' or even 'healthy' in the process of industrialisation has for long been noted. In general, as these adjectives imply, this persistence has been seen as a negative feature. From Gramsci onwards, many writers have tended to underline what they see to be the undesirable economic consequences of the failure to implement agrarian reform after Unification. Emilio Sereni, for example, emphasises the retarding effects on the process of economic change in Italy of what he terms 'feudal residues' in agriculture, suggesting that antiquated contracts and proprietorial absenteeism represented a dead weight on the economy.[6] From this point of view, fundamentally critical of the Risorgimento process, the absence of modernisation in much of Italian agriculture is considered to have created an obstacle to the industrialisation of Italy. Agriculture, which *through its development* should have generated the funds for industry, failed to do so; the survival of an area of peasant subsistence agriculture is simply the reverse side of this failure. This is so in particular for those looking for a definitive separation of a great part of the rural population from the land on the example of the English farm-workers at the time of the agricultural revolution.

Of course, the 'late comer' model, with rapid industrialisation 'from above' and forced accumulation from agriculture on the one hand, and rural stagnation on the other, goes some way to meet these arguments. Even so, comparisons with other models are risky; the result has often been the tendency to identify Italian 'failures' rather than to assess the significance of a different pattern of transformation. A more flexible approach, which concentrates less on accumulation than on the development of relations of production, may provide a more instructive picture. In the Comasco and Alto Milanese, the evolution of the peasant–worker family suggests that some aspects of Italian industrialisation were more gradual than is generally assumed for a 'late comer'. The obstinate refusal of many rural families to conform to the traditional model of industrialisation and leave the land is indeed a characteristic of many areas of northern Italy – but this did not necessarily interrupt or retard the process of industrialisation, as some would have it. Rather, *the specific feature of industrialisation in such areas would appear to be precisely the long period in which agricultural and industrial employment was combined within the same household – and, by extension, within the local community.* This had benefits which went well beyond the accumulation of capital for big industry. We suggest, in fact, that this combination of activity – this ability on the part of families to fudge the issue of choice between total commitment to either sector – has in the end represented a strength rather than a weakness for the Italian economy, and should be judged an element of economic dynamism rather than an indication of economic backwardness.[7]

The influences – opportunity, convenience, political culture, social attitudes – which determine the evolution of peasant families in the direction of entrepreneurship will be examined in the course of this work. Certain points stand out, however, and it may be a useful guide to the reader to anticipate them here in general terms. It is important to note that the transformation involved a gradual change in family outlook – from that of an economic unit whose principal aim was that of survival (i.e. the reproduction of the family unit in the Kautskyian sense), to that of a unit able to some extent to assess economic alternatives and make decisions on the basis of that assessment. That this change depended on the existence of alternatives to the agriculture-silk cycle is clear (the process of the evolution of peasant outlook is not necessarily autonomous, therefore); but it is equally clear that the kind of work involved in that cycle, and the division of roles within the family, made the peasant family particularly receptive to these alternatives. In accepting them, the static model of family survival at subsistence level was replaced by a dynamic model of capital accumulation, land purchase, and economic enterprise. This was not the classic 'freeing of labour' from agriculture for industrial work; rather it was a new definition of the interweaving of activity in which both the basic agricultural income and non-agricultural earnings remained essential for integration of family introits.

The variations on this model are many, depending on a whole variety of factors – for example, on family size, on the extent of the holding, or on the proximity to industry. One factor remains constant, however. Critical to the process of transition was the division of roles within the family. What people did was, in a sense, less important than *who* did what. The clear allocation of economic roles was the feature which permitted, first, survival on the land, and, subsequently, expansion into other forms of activity. Men dominated the rural family household; their social and political culture, which derived in large part from their economic activity, determined prevailing attitudes within the family. Where men remained fully employed in agriculture, therefore, their conservative and patriarchal outlook (the region was predominantly Catholic, but that was not the only factor in determining conservatism) was likely to outweigh the more subversive tendencies of their wives and daughters – the female factory workers. If men moved to factory work, even on a seasonal basis, the situation could become very different. Gender in relation to economic activity, changing roles within the family over the decades, and attitudes to economic opportunity (usually the dominant male attitudes) thus constitute key points in our argument.

As will already be obvious, diffused rural industry and pluriactivity produced a workforce which had little in common with the urban proletariat of Great Britain, Germany, or even Turin. The peasant–worker family was a social form of production based on the division of roles between *different* sectors of activity, on the extremely careful organisation of family

time, and on the awareness of the need for integration of income
from non-agricultural sources for survival. That such families did
not follow the classic road towards proletarianisation is
surprising only if one assumes a ri~~gid~~ model for development of
~~both indust~~   *why* families did not leave

~~one of the centr~~al questions of this book.
~~We aim to show th~~at ~~the~~ ~~context of~~ the silk-mill and the Alto
~~Milanese. pr~~   ~~anisation provided no
~~ems – as long as other
~~ly because of a peasant
~~the land (such a culture
did not prevent massive
context of a rapidly
the social form of the
~~ter security at critical
es at others than did a

~~olitical culture. In fact,
workers – after 1900,
~~th a political and social
~~ased, full-time factory
ction of the culture of
the impact of factory
s (and, in many cases,
shock represented by
~~ant–worker families
reflected the fact that
nomic independence
~~ne family. It was a
maximising earnings,
~~ude of minimising
and a piece of land
dustry was a major
~~economy. As we shall see, cultural
factors play a central role in pushing the family towards
entrepreneurship.

What we have tried to do in this study is identify and examine
the characteristics of this specific social form. In a number of
ways the peasant–worker family represented a very flexible
unit, adaptable to opportunity, and, in turn, increasingly
entrepreneurial in spirit (in the sense of seeking out the best

opportunities, organising time, and exploiting skills learned in dependent employment). As will become clear, these qualities, combined with the traditional peasant qualities of astuteness, even cunning, acquired in dealing with the landlord, were likely to make the peasant family a particularly effective economic unit.

To speak of peasant families and rural manufactures inevitably raises the issue of protoindustrialisation, and it is perhaps necessary to explain briefly why we have decided not to follow the model provided by protoindustrial theory. Certainly, many of the features which form the basis of the protoindustrialisation thesis are present in the areas of silk-production – domestic industry, putting out, etc. This has persuaded at least one writer that large areas of the hill zones of northern Italy can be included in the protoindustrial model, precisely because of the general intertwining of agricultural and industrial activity among peasant families.[8] It is true, of course, that domestic industry was for long characteristic of the hill areas of the Alto Milanese, even if it had declined considerably by the middle of the nineteenth century. But the subsequent history of the region suggests that there are problems with the protoindustrial interpretation when it is related to the silk industry.

Protoindustrial theory tends to posit a series of phases, and the intertwining of agricultural and industrial activity is only one such phase. The others are the separation of the worker from the land, the establishment of urban factories and the formation of an urban proletariat. All this can be demonstrated to have happened in the Milan area, but it is not the central feature of developments in those areas where rural families were involved with silk. Peasant families certainly sent workers to the factories, but it is significant that the factories moved from the towns to the countryside (in 1850 two large factories in Milan dominated silk-production; those factories had moved away from the centre by 1880) and that labour was in fact tied to the land, (or enabled to survive on the land) because of the possibility of non-agricultural earnings. Rather than speeding a gradual process towards a centralised, large-scale industry in the region in the period before 1914, silk-production seems to have blocked precisely such a development, creating diffused industry over a wide area, but not dissolving the tight links between agricultural activity and industrial labour.

Certain explanations of this phenomenon will be outlined below, in Chapters 2 and 3; here at the outset, perhaps, it is worth noting that silk was in some ways unique – and not only in the sense that it was a semi-'industrial' agricultural product. Unlike many other Italian industries at the end of the last century, in European terms the silk industry was a leader in its field rather than a follower. Italian silk *dominated* its market before the First World War. Silk did not have to modify its structure continually and create larger units in order to meet the competition of more advanced industrial countries. On the contrary, until the First World War, those changes which were implemented were made in order to augment production because of increased demand from abroad. In other words, the Italian industry was not compelled to imitate the structures of foreign counterparts and could therefore determine to some extent its own pace of change. In addition, a high population density in the region meant that labour bottlenecks were never an incentive to change the structure of industry. As a consequence, the relationship between peasant family and industrial production remained very much the same until the War, with neither 'industrialisation' in the generally accepted sense of the word (concentration, urbanisation), nor 'de-industrialisation' in the protoindustrial sense a result of the lack of change.

Indeed, the significant moment of departure from the protoindustrial model occurs precisely at the point at which the silk industry begins to decline – that is, in the years between the two World Wars, when increased costs of production and competition from the Far East finally combined to undermine the Italian position. The decline of silk might seem to invite arguments about 'de-industrialisation'; after all, it would seem, diffused, rurally-based manufacturing could not make it. On the contrary, from the end of the 1920s, the Como region sees a considerable expansion of new small businesses. Surprisingly, many rurally-based families began to demonstrate some kind of entrepreneurship through the formation of small and independent activities – the phenomenon which lies at the centre of this book. Many such businesses were undoubtedly created by a provincial bourgeoisie grown rich over the years through the silk trade or through sales of land after the first conflict, or by the well-consolidated class of local artisans – both groups who could make good use of relatively cheap and abundant peasant labour.

But some new small businesses were the product of initiatives of peasant-worker families who remained in some way connected to agriculture and the land. The pattern of diffused industry was maintained, therefore, even with the collapse of silk. Central to this process was, of course, the peasant family – both as workforce, and, on occasions, as the source of potential entrepreneurs. As will be shown in Chapter 5, the first indications of entrepreneurship which emerged in the inter-war years were to be confirmed by the much greater development in small businesses in the period following the Second World War.

For these reasons, it seems to us that the pattern of employment established by the silk industry, and the social forms which the industry produced, correspond better to the definition of pluriactivity (an ugly word, but a useful concept) than to that of protoindustrialisation. The former term describes more a pattern of behaviour than a historical process, and is in a sense less interesting, therefore. Nevertheless, the concept of pluriactivity – in the sense of the willingness of the individual, or the family as a unit, to engage in more than one activity across sectors in order to integrate relatively low individual income – describes fairly accurately the situation of the peasant–worker families between the nineteenth and twentieth centuries. The straddling of the two sectors was the critical factor, first in survival, and then in accumulation. And it was this accumulation which permitted the purchase of land in the first place, and in the second, in some cases, entry into small-scale manufacturing. Moreover, pluriactivity determined the structure and distribution of industry. Continued dependence on the land by the workforce ensured that industry was territorially dispersed and that industrial concentration did not take place.

The relative economic advantages of diffused industry and a pluriactive population will be examined in more detail below. The key factor, which it is worth emphasising from the outset, was undoubtedly the availability of cheap and plentiful labour during the development and consolidation of the structure. The heavy exploitation of peasant labour in the factories was the price peasant families paid; and because of the system of dual introits for the family, landowners were also able to increase the level of exploitation of farm-work. The peasant family survived, therefore, through massive inputs of labour. In the nineteenth century this was a necessity; in the twentieth it appears to have become something of a habit. The enormous efforts which were made, initially for survival, were subsequently channelled into accumulation, and then into the search for autonomy in both agriculture and small business. And in the last case long hours remained equally important for success. The high level of 'self-exploitation' of the head of the family, and of exploitation of the rest of the family and other relations, may explain why size of family remained a crucial factor. It was less possible to require the same kind of commitment from non-family labour – which tended, therefore, to represent an increase in costs disproportionate to the increase in production.

On a wider front, the study of the pluriactive family and of the passage from peasant to entrepreneur invites some reflections on the overall process of industrialisation in Italy. As is well known, this is something of a delicate subject. The debates which have surrounded the interpretations of Gramsci, Romeo and Gerschenkron will be familiar to many. The concepts of passive revolution, primitive accumulation, and 'big spurt' have inhabited the pages of economic histories for a long time. Here we are less concerned with what are essentially macroeconomic arguments than with the identification of a social group which has contributed greatly to industrialisation over a long period of time. In a sense, we slightly side-step the role of banks, railways, and the State in order to watch a different process which – if not always autonomous – often seems to run parallel to the formation of big industry.

The identification of this different process is, of course, not without its implications for the story of Italian industrialisation. As has already been suggested, attention to historical models of industrialisation has served perhaps to direct the interest of researchers towards the construction of the heavy industries on the one hand and urbanisation and the proletarianisation of the workforce on the other. Yet the Comasco, which has been a significant industrial area for well over a hundred years, has seen none of these developments. The area which – through silk – provided the principal 'occasion'[9] for the further industrialisation of Italy through the contribution it made to the balance of payments during the formative years, itself remained relatively unscathed by the formation of the industrial triangle. It conserved its diffused industrial structure and its pluriactive workforce through different phases of industrialisation, responding to both crisis and opportunity with a kind of logic which was internal to the region rather than assumed from outside.

In this last respect it is worth noting that the evolution of the Comasco and the industrialisation of the region has been anything but typical of a 'late comer'. The creation of the nation state, which might have provided a stimulus through an extension of the market for silk, did little or nothing for the industry, already orientated in other directions. Indeed, it has been suggested that silk would probably have managed better without Unification.[10] Equally the State, usually seen as the motor of the process of late development, is largely absent. It provided neither finance nor orders; its trading policies often damaged the local industry; and it had to do almost nothing to maintain discipline among the working population. No doubt these considerations reflect the fact that the region, as a province of the Habsburg Empire, was already a part of the economic hub of Europe before 1860 and had market links and social structures to match. The intervention of the State in support of industry was therefore less necessary. Even so, the relative autonomy of the industrialisation process which was apparent in the years following Unification has remained the distinctive feature of the region throughout its various phases of development, just as it is the independent initiative and enterprise of rural families which would appear to characterise many of the success stories of the Third Italy.

State-fostered industries are, in reality, only a part of the picture of Italian industrialisation, and concentration on them leaves much unexplained. Our aim is to examine this separate line of development – sometimes related to big industry, sometimes not. Above all we seek to demonstrate that the small businesses of the Comasco were not destined from their foundation to become big businesses, just as the small businesses of the Third Italy are not necessarily a product of the problems of large-scale mass production. Many small businesses, both past and present, conform in fact to a different logic which renders them neither backward nor anomalous, but simply highly successful examples of a specific form of social and economic development.

In the first sections of this book we look in particular at the evolution of the social form of the worker–peasant family, examining the development of relations between farming families and rural industries over the course of more than a century. The later sections attempt to bring the argument up to date through an examination of the development and the precise nature of the small industries formed after the Second World War, through a look at the growth of industrial districts on Marshallian lines, and through a commentary on some of the existing literature on the Third Italy, which is revisited in the light of the historical perspective offered here.

Notes

1. The original definition of the concept of the 'Third Italy' is to be found in A. Bagnasco, *Tre Italie. La problematica territoriale dello sviluppo italiano*, Bologna 1977.

2. There is now a considerable literature on this subject, to which reference will be made in the course of the text. But see, in particular, M. Paci, *La struttura sociale italiana*, Bologna 1982; S. Brusco, *Agricoltura ricca e classi sociali*, Milan 1979; C. Trigilia, *Grandi partiti e piccole inprese: comunisti e democristiani nelle regioni a economia diffusa*, Bologna 1986. Specifically on the question of historical models, se D. Landes (ed.), *A che servono i padroni? Le alternative storiche dell'industrializzazione*, Turin 1987, which debates the issues raised in the article of C. Sabel and J. Zeitlin, 'Historical alternatives to mass production: politics, markets and technology in nineteenth century industrialisation', *Past and Present*, CVIII, 1985.

3. The most comprehensive work on the silk industry and its implications for Italian economic development is L. Cafagna, *Dualismo e sviluppo nella storia d'Italia*, Venice 1989.

4. G. Procacci, *La lotta di classe in Italia agli inizi del secolo XX*, Rome 1970; S. Merli, *Proletariato di fabbrica e capitalismo industriale. Il caso italiano 1880–1900*, Florence 1972.

5. See A. De Clementi, 'Appunti sulla formazione della classe operaia in Italia', in *Studi storici*, 32, 1976; P. Villani, 'La storia sociale: problemi e prospettive di ricerca', in *Storia d'Italia Einaudi*, Annali 1, 1979.

6. E. Sereni, *Il capitalismo nelle campagne*, Turin 1947.

7. P. Corner, *Dall'agricoltura all'industria*, Milan 1992, Introduzione.

8. A. Dewerpe, *L'industrie aux champs. Essai sur la protoindustrialisation en Italie du Nord (1800–1880)*, Rome 1985.

9. The term is used by Cafagna (*Dualismo e sviluppo*) to indicate those few

factors which operated in favour of Italian industrialisation during the last century.

10. Cafagna, *Dualismo e sviluppo*, p. XXVII.

2
Peasant Families and Rural Labour
1815–1890

2.1. Grain Rents, Silk, and Peasant Poverty

The Lombardy of the Risorgimento was a region already characterised by profound transformations in its social and economic structure. Indeed, it could be argued that the changes which had taken place in the century before Italian unification were more radical than were those which were to occur in the century which followed. Land reclamation, irrigation, the introduction of high farming (crop rotation, meadows, livestock) on the plains – all of which was both a consequence of a keen business sense among Lombard proprietors and a stimulus to further enterprise – had served to make the agriculture of certain zones of Lombardy among the richest in Europe – a fact which was widely recognised at the time by foreign visitors.[1]

Not all areas of the region were involved in these changes to the same extent, however. In the hill regions above Milan – an area which comprised the Alto Milanese, the Brianza, and the Comasco – and in the more mountainous country further to the north, the land was dry, less fertile and more difficult to work.[2] Those incentives to investment and transformation which had so changed the plains were absent; pouring money into the land simply did not produce the same kind of returns for landowners, most of whom only visited their properties during the summer months in any case. Natural barriers to increased production combined with human obstacles in such a way as to produce a vicious circle. The poor quality of forage, and, more important, the difficulty of cultivating meadows on the dry land of the hills, made it expensive and difficult to rear livestock. This in turn forced the peasant to rely almost exclusively on vegetable silage, less satisfactory than that produced by animals, which in turn affected the degree to which farmers could rotate crops and alternate arable with fallow. In addition, the sharecroppers of the hill regions could not be compared, in terms of wealth, with the capitalist leaseholders of the large estates of the plains. The capital required to invest in livestock on a worthwhile scale in an attempt to improve the fertility of the land had to come, therefore, from the landowner rather than the tenant. But, as is well known, livestock represented the biggest risk in farming at this time because of the high incidence of epidemics. Consequently landowners quickly abandoned any idea of basing changes in production in the hill areas on the kind of land improvement which, along with other more natural advantages, had served to make the plains such a prosperous area.[3]

The landed proprietors of the hill regions were left facing a problem which had no obvious solution. A relatively slow, extensive agriculture, based on regular ploughing and the sowing of grain crops, beans, and vegetables appeared to promise little for proprietors; wine was likely to be the most saleable product of the land. It was only at the end of the eighteenth century that this situation saw a sudden and dramatic change.[4] Between 1770 and 1780 wheat prices increased significantly in the whole of Europe, and the Lombard landowners of the hill regions saw their opportunity. Their chances of wealth depended on increasing both the production of wheat and the share which was allotted to them. The extensive farming typical of the region was not particularly well adapted to this kind of change; as a result proprietors began to look for an intensification of production through changes in the system of cultivation. New contracts were stipulated with peasant families, who now had the task of growing as much wheat as possible on the small piece of land assigned to them. This required intensive cultivation with the hoe and very high inputs of labour. Grain production was increased in this way, but an adverse consequence was that this was achieved by encroaching on meadows and fallow and reducing further the number of livestock animals. The dangers of soil exhaustion were thus extended.

The contracts between peasants and proprietors, based on the production of a high volume of grain, introduced an element of instability into the agriculture of the region which could not have persisted – on the same terms – for long. The very intensive cultivation of land induced peasants to have large families in order to meet labour requirements; but this strategy was somewhat self-defeating, in as far as more peasants meant that more food was needed. Population in the region increased dramatically, a fact which further increased pressure on the land. After they had satisfied the requirements of the contract of tenure, peasants were left with very little. In fact they became poorer and poorer, and moved towards what was essentially subsistence farming.

The final crisis of the system appeared to have arrived at the time of the Restoration, when grain prices suddenly plummeted. Instead, proprietors – facing disaster – were saved by the rapid rise in the price of another product typical of the hill regions – raw silk. Silkworms had always been raised by peasants on a small scale, and the cocoons were usually divided on a 50/50 basis with the proprietor, with the peasants selling the rest in order to realise a spare-time subsidiary income.[5] Occasional upward oscillations in silk prices had produced short-lived silk crazes on the part of landowners; the so-called *bacomania* (from *baco* – the silkworm) of the whole of the Milanese at the beginning of the nineteenth century was one such phase.[6] But if *bacomania* was confined to a few years, the consistent demand for raw silk induced more and more proprietors to take the production of silk cocoons seriously. In the 1820s and 1830s prices rose by more than 100 per cent (to the extent that Cattaneo was provoked into writing that 'we ourselves are astonished and almost frightened by it') and production more than doubled.[7] By the late 1840s, Lombardy–Venetia was the principal exporter of raw silk to the rest of Europe, with an annual production of more than 5 million pounds in weight.[8] The great increase in foreign demand led to the total transformation of the hill regions, as the mulberry tree extended its shade over vast tracts of territory. For landowners silk had become the passport to wealth; as was said at the time, 'the shade of the mulberry is the shade of gold'. Land prices increased accordingly.[9]

The way in which the hill regions adjusted to this priority was to be of crucial importance for the future of the population involved in silk production. The very high value of silk on international markets might have been expected to induce landowners to scrap the old wheat-based contracts and turn everything over to silk. Virtual subsistence farming, with the contradictions inherent in it, could have been replaced by industrial farming directed principally towards what was an immensely valuable cash crop. For reasons which are difficult to identify precisely, but not hard to guess, landowners rejected this line forward.[10] The agrarian reform – in reality a complete change of system – which such a step required would have been costly and the social consequences uncertain. Moreover, despite its promise of riches, silk remained a high-risk product because of the frequent outbreak of disease. The complete revision of the agricultural system in the hills in favour of silk and the mulberry tree represented, therefore, an investment with aspects of risk which landowners were unwilling to accept. Particularly when there was another – less risky – way to achieve much the same result.

Instead of replacing wheat production with silk, proprietors decided – almost from the start of the boom – to integrate the new crop with the old. Silk was grafted on to the *existing* system, even if it did eventually come to dominate it. In reality, if the combination of wheat and silk was not logically the most profitable path to pursue, wheat and silk production were not intrinsically (i.e. agronomically) in contradiction with each other – providing certain conditions were observed. These conditions concerned essentially the relationship between landowner and peasant family and involved the central feature of this relationship – the contract.

Existing contracts – those which had been introduced to take advantage of the rise in grain prices – had already had the effect of determining profound changes in the social structure of the region. Before 1770, families in the region had traditionally been very large, multiple, families, sometimes comprising five or six married couples with their accompanying in-laws, children, etc.[11] A 'family' of forty persons was not unusual. The family was rigidly patriarchal, controlled by one man – called variously the *capo*, *capoccia* or *reggitore* – whose authority was rarely contested, and it was with the *capoccia* that the proprietor stipulated the contract of sharecropping which concerned the entire family.[12] In return for a rent-free house, peasants would normally hand over around half the production of saleable goods such as wine and silk cocoons, and would also provide a fixed amount of grain.

This was a system not altogether dissimilar to that of the Tuscan *mezzadria*, and it had many of the same characteristics. Paternalism was the basis of the landlord's relationship with the peasants; but it was a paternalism which also guaranteed stability (contracts were usually renewed tacitly on a three- or a nine-year basis) and relative prosperity. The plots of land allocated to extended families were large – up to 25 hectares – and the sprawling farm houses (the *massaricia*, which gave its name to the entire system of *masseria*) adequate for the numbers of people involved. Indeed, there was an unwritten but nonetheless firmly understood agreement between landlord and extended family that land and accommodation should broadly match the needs of the family. There were also the same causes of resentment as in Tuscany. Peasants were expected to provide certain gifts for the proprietor at certain times of the year (eggs, cheese, poultry) and to work unpaid, or for very little pay, for a few days a year on the land used directly by the proprietor (these obligations were the so-called *appendizi* or *giornate d'obbligo*). This last condition is perhaps the best indication of the antiquated nature of this kind of sharecropping contract.[13]

Changes provoked by the rise in grain prices altered in fundamental ways both the relationships within the family and those with the proprietor. The decision to intensify production by dividing up some of the larger farms and making contracts with individual nuclear families (called *pigionanti* – literally 'renters') provoked a disintegration of the old patriarchal family in many cases and led to the establishment – alongside those wealthier *massari* who remained[14] – of a new class of desperately poor workers. The *pigionanti* possessed no capital and none of the means of production (except for their hoes) and were in effect little more than dependent labourers. They had few means of defence against the innovations of the landowner. The multiple family had possessed certain of the means of production – the oxen and the plough, for example – and this had given the *capoccia* some authority in his dealings with the proprietor. In addition, it was clearly not easy for the proprietor to replace the multiple family with another; large family groups did not move easily from one farm to another. Landowners knew this, and would think twice before refusing to renew contracts. But by ignoring the *capoccia* and dealing directly with the smaller family units, the proprietor put himself in a much stronger position. Individual families could be evicted and replaced with much greater ease. In a region of high population density, such as the Brianza, peasants were undoubtedly well aware of this. Loss of land through a failure to arrive at a renewal of contract could only constitute a disaster.

The gradual breakdown of many of the multiple, patriarchal, families, the sub-division of farms, the worsening contractual terms – all served to replace security with insecurity, and a measure of prosperity with poverty. As the new contract – the mixed grain rent (*fitto misto a grano*) – became better-defined and was extended to most of the hill region, its implications became ever more clear. Annual renewal, in the place of three- or nine-year contracts, discouraged peasants from long-term planning and encouraged heavy short-term exploitation of woods and fields. The fact that peasants were now expected to produce a greater quantity of wheat for rent resulted in their having to sow around two-thirds of the plot to wheat for the proprietor, leaving them little land for production for their own consumption.[15] Peasants reacted to this by relying more and more on maize, which had high yields when compared with wheat, but which was unsatisfactory from a dietary point of view. The persistence of pellagra in the region throughout the century is adequate testimony of this.[16]

The contractual changes had even more fundamental implications for the peasant economy. Family size had usually been determined, at least in part, by the agricultural cycle, which required large amounts of labour at certain times of the year and relatively little at others. It was normal for peasant families to find themselves with little to do in the winter months – a time they traditionally devoted to domestic industry. Security for the family lay in establishing a reasonable level of equilibrium between employment and inactivity, between production and consumption. Contractual changes and new emphases in production threatened to disturb this balance. As we have already seen, the heavy labour requirements of the wheat contract tended to produce large families. This situation was accentuated by the increasing importance given to silk, because the raising of the worms and the gathering of the mulberry leaves imposed great demands on the family for a few weeks in the early summer.[17] The more landed proprietors put the emphasis of production on silk, therefore, the more they tended to create a situation in which large families were maintained in order to satisfy the labour requirements of a very short period of time and of a product which paid the rent, but did nothing to help the family materially (in the sense of filling the larder) through the winter. Structural unemployment in agriculture thus became a feature of the area and tended to develop along with the accentuation of cereal culture and the growth of silk-production. With this unemployment came the risk that the essential balance within the peasant family between producers and consumers had been radically upset.

A consequence of this was a great increase in peasant debt. Peasants were obliged to take more from the landowner at the beginning of the year than they were able to repay at the end. This was in reality an essential part of the system from the point of view of the landowner. Indeed, peasant debt was the factor which permitted landowners to square the circle of maintaining antiquated social relations implied by cereal culture without losing the advantages of enormously valuable silk-production. As a result of debt, peasants would hand over all the cocoons to the proprietor, which would then be set against what was owed.[18] In this way landowners managed to appropriate all of an extraordinarily profitable crop without being compelled to realise expensive changes in the system of production. They were also paid their grain and any other marketable products, as stipulated by the contract. It was a system of almost total expropriation of the products of farming. In this way peasants became almost entirely excluded from the market (this had inevitable consequences on the development of production in the region which grew to rely on exportable produce because of the weakness of local demand).[19] A high level of production, and of capital accumulation, was thus realised on the basis of a low level of consumption. During the course of the nineteenth century landowners consistently increased the level of pressure on the peasants, requiring greater quantities of wheat and more and more cocoons. The threat of eviction was sufficient to keep peasant families in line.

Observers of the situation in northern Lombardy in the middle of the nineteenth century agreed that peasant families really lived below what would normally have been regarded as the level of subsistence. In general, patrician agronomists were concerned about peasant poverty but were obviously inclined to blame the peasants themselves. They were seen as intensely conservative, stubborn and diffident in their attitudes to possible changes in methods of cultivation of the land.[20] Often it was assumed that a solution lay in the instruction of the peasants, and in the first half of the century there were numerous initiatives which aimed at the establishment of schools or other means of instruction which were intended to open the eyes of the peasants to the possibilities of scientific farming.[21] But by the 1850s it was becoming clear that instruction was not the answer to the problem. Stefano Jacini, the foremost Lombard agronomist of the period, was one of the first to recognise the limitations – from a purely agronomic point of view – of the wheat rent. His comments reveal the extent to which, in effect, the peasant was tied hand and foot to the provision of grain and silk for the proprietor. Any initiatives, which might well fail, could see the peasant hopelessly indebted and dispossessed. As Jacini wrote, '... where this system of cultivation is predominant, it is pointless to expect experiments or new agricultural practices, or the application of scientific improvements, and agriculture stays in a state of immobility as it has for centuries'. Subsistence farming excluded any prospect of peasant improvement through specialisation for the market – again, the risks were too great. Short-term contracts not only discouraged initiative; the contract even impeded rational farming. Mario Romani, writing of the grain rent, notes that '... in the agronomic literature criticisms [of the contract] are general because of the wretched conditions it imposes on peasants, and because of the obstacles it places in the way of agricultural progress'.[22]

Obviously proprietors were not going to change an extremely profitable system as long as silk continued to give them what they wanted. Large profits in this area could cover a multitude of sins in any other. Peasants thus found themselves essentially victims of silk. It was a product which, on the one hand, forced them to live with extremely harsh contracts and a labour-intensive style of farming, and which, on the other, distracted the interest of the proprietor from any changes in the methods of cultivation.

The very high return on investment which silk provided served to accelerate the tendencies towards revision of agricultural contracts and subdivision of land. From the 1820s on, landowners began to think almost entirely in terms of cocoon production and left other aspects of farming to the peasants themselves. They – the landowners – moved to the towns[23] and left clear instructions to their factors: 'Make sure the peasant hands over the cocoons and the wheat which are due to me. I can't be bothered about the rest; he can take care of that.'[24]

Peasants suffered under the pressure, and the story of the nineteenth century would appear to be that of a steady worsening of already bad conditions for most peasant families. People found it impossible not to comment on the fact that, in the area which was producing one of the most valuable agricultural commodities, the peasants should be among the poorest in Europe.[25] In reality, of course, peasant poverty and high returns from silk were the reverse sides of the same coin. Only the breakdown of the old patriarchal system and the subdivision of land permitted the kind of intensive cultivation of the territory which the wheat rent demanded and the mulberry tree required; the same breakdown of the old system ensured that peasants remained indebted, isolated from the market, and unable to benefit from the wealth they were instrumental in creating.

2.2. Peasant Families and Rural Manufacturing

The peasant families who survived in this situation of extremely high exploitation did so only because they were able to supplement agricultural income from other forms of work. This was not simply a matter of part-time domestic industry. While domestic industry had for long been common in peasant households, it had rarely assumed a position of crucial importance in the economy of the multiple family. The spinning of silk thread, weaving, woodwork and basketwork – these were all activities which had served to occupy peasant families during the winter months, and their characteristics had been that they were spare-time, compatibile with the agricultural cycle, and often performed within the home. But it was not this kind of activity which had come to the assistance of increasingly impoverished peasant families. At least from the middle of the eighteenth century – probably from much before – peasants had begun to leave the land for certain periods of the year in order to work in factories. Certain of the processes involved in the production of raw silk, for example, had been centralised since before 1700. The silk 'mill' was no new phenomenon, nor were sheds which employed rudimentary processes to produce paper, to treat leather, or to make bricks. Around Lecco, to the west of the region, metalworking was also a traditional occupation, with guns a speciality.[26]

Initially, the factories which developed grew up within the towns or immediately outside, and in general the first peasants to be employed in these manufactures were those from the mountainous areas of the region where, if families sometimes even owned the land they worked, limited farm size and poor land fertility made survival extremely difficult. Certain members of these families would descend for a few weeks or a few months in order to supplement the family income through what was essentially a kind of internal emigration.[27] Such employment could generally be accommodated to the requirements of the land.

It was the expansion of the silk industry which transformed this pattern during the first half of the nineteenth century. The early silk-mills had been involved principally in the production of yarn which could then be woven. This involved twisting threads from the unravelled cocoon in order to increase their strength (a process known as *torcitura*).[28] The process of unravelling – the throwing and winding – had usually been done by the peasants at home. It was regarded as an integral part of the business of raising silkworms. Small factories involved in *torcitura* had spread across much of the mountainous area of the north-east of the region after 1800. They relied on local labour and were often virtually single-family operations, working for a part of the year only.[29] The gradual mechanisation of the spinning process during the first half of the nineteenth century served to destroy even this aspect of the domestic industry, however. The spinning factories – the *filande* – developed rapidly throughout the region, using wood-fired vats of water to provide the steam to loosen the silk, and simple winding-machines which relied on people turning handles, or occasionally on basic types of steam engine. Initially they were usually small production units, essentially artisanal, although there are records of factories employing more than 100 workers in the Lecco region as early as 1808.[30]

From the middle of the century, and with increasing pace after the outbreaks of silkworm disease in the 1850s,[31] the structure and location of the industry began to change. The myriad small units in the mountainous areas of the region began to be replaced by larger, mechanised, factories, which made much greater use of steam power. And whereas before 1850 the tendency had been for production of yarn to be based either in the poorer mountain areas or in the towns and their suburbs, the second half of the century saw a move to the hill valleys and away from the original centres of production. As Greenfield writes, 'the manufacturing industry of the region was widely and increasingly diffused through the countryside',[32] while Jacini noted that 'manufacturing activity in our region, passing from the wool to the silk mills, has largely abandoned the towns and has come to settle in the countryside'.[33] Even Milan, for example, which had been a centre of production in the 1840s, lost this role by 1870 and specialised instead on the commercial operations involved.[34]

This concentration of the industry into larger units – a certain process of vertical integration appears to have taken place – and the diffusion of these units through the hill valleys was determined by several factors. It was in the hill valleys of Como and the Brianza that *fabbricanti* (the factory owners) could find ample supplies of water and wood, essential to the creation of the steam employed in the unwinding of the cocoons and the twisting of the thread, and the move to the countryside also put them in closer contact with their raw material.[35] In these years of the mid-century many factory owners were still also landowners. By building factories on their own land they were better able to control all stages of production of the silk thread. In particular, they could dominate the local market for cocoons, fix what were really notional prices (i.e. based on their own valuation of what was advanced to the peasant at the beginning of the year) to their own advantage, and avoid what all landowners feared – the secret subtraction of cocoons for private sale on the part of the peasants.

But the principal factor in determining the shift to rural production was undoubtedly the availability of the right kind of labour. Indeed, the availability of labour of the right type and at the right price (i.e. the lowest price) was unquestionably the key to the rapid development of the silk industry in the hill valleys of the region. That such labour was available was a direct result of the changes in the agricultural structure which had been witnessed since the middle of the previous century. The patriarchal family of the *massaricia* had been able to survive without recourse to anything other than agricultural activities, helped out from time to time by a little domestic textile production. On the whole, agricultural production – even under terms of sharecropping and the division of produce – had accounted for the needs of the family. Landowners and peasant families adjusted their thinking in order to realise the appropriate balance between the land and the people who lived on it. As we have seen, the wheat rent, which did so much to worsen the conditions of peasant life, had upset this stability. Overpopulation in respect of the agricultural possibilities of the region, insecurity of tenure, and simple poverty combined to push peasant workers towards the factories. Members of *pigionanti* families were obliged to take other opportunities when they occurred; as a consequence, they began to compete in the search for work in the silk factories in an attempt to compensate for the loss of income which contractual change and mechanisation of peasant industries had provoked in peasant households.

After a brief initial phase in which men worked for short periods each year in the silk-mills, those who went to the factories were almost entirely women and children, who increasingly worked on a virtually full-time basis. They seemed to provide what was in many respects the perfect workforce. Their labour was extremely cheap, because the employer did not feel responsibile for paying for housing or even food, and because there was competition for work. The workforce was also extremely flexible; in times of crisis workers could be sent back to agricultural employment without notice, or simply not employed at all in a bad year. The reservoir of labour remained, to be utilised in better times. Protest was unlikely. A major factor in favour of peasant labour (from the point of view of the employer) was that female and child workers were considered politically 'docile', whereas male workers might create problems. Peasant factory workers thus represented a particularly convenient form of labour. They were part of an agricultural community, and therefore 'fixed' to the land; but their family circumstances meant that they were also 'free' to work in rural manufacturing.[36]

This adaptation of the existing sharecropping system, which rested on the grain rent, to the needs of silk-production – the 'grafting on' of the new to the old referred to above – represented the triumph of a certain kind of proprietorial policy. The agricultural requirements of immensely increased silk-production were met, not by agrarian reform, but by putting more pressure on individual peasant families. That pressure – in turn – created the workforce for the industrial requirements of the same silk industry. The interdependence of these two facets of activity – agricultural and industrial – was so perfect that, for a long time, landowners and industrialists saw little reason to change a highly profitable arrangement. Peasants, of course, had little choice in the matter. And indeed, little was changed in the relationship between peasant families and silk for more than half a century. As early as the middle of the century, one writer had spoken of a system of production which was 'mesmerised by its own success'.[37] This impression remained. The interweaving of agriculture and industry served to create a situation of immobility which was to persist almost until silk itself ceased to be profitable.

The industrialisation of the hill regions was realised, therefore, without the expulsion of labour from agriculture. Even less was it realised through the full employment of labour in a dynamic, expanding, agriculture, which paved the way for industry. Silk permitted proprietors to avoid the patterns of rural transition which had taken place elsewhere; the contribution of rural labour to industrialisation was different as well, therefore. As Luciano Cafagna has written, 'That condition of industrial development provided by the support of rural labour to industry, which in other countries is realised through the classic form of the agrarian revolution, is here realised by avoiding that revolution'.[38]

2.3. Women's Labour and Peasant Survival

The depositions given in 1870 to the *Inchiesta industriale* – the first national enquiry after unification into the condition of Italian industry – provide ample evidence of the convenience of peasant labour for industrialists. Cost was a factor referred to again and again. Workers were not totally dependent for survival on their wages; the industrialists could take advantage of this situation: '... the women employed here in Lombardy in the mills belong for nine tenths to peasant families. For these families the wage earned by the women in the factory does not represent their only means of subsistence, but is simply a complementary income. For this reason they settle for pay which would be inadequate if they were forced to live exclusively with that.'[39] Equally, peasant labour was slow to organise against bad conditions. Competition for jobs was such that strikes turned into lockouts very quickly. On many occasions factory owners dismissed the entire workforce, knowing that they would have no difficulty in finding new workers. One owner's response to attempts at labour organisation was typical: 'At Valmadrera many of the workers in the spinning works belonged to the infamous society of Lecco. I decided to send them all home in April of 1869, replacing them with girls from other villages. The example worked wonderfully.'[40]

Rural poverty and desperation were obviously the preconditions of peasant contact with manufacturing. This is clear from any number of contemporary accounts. Conditions in rural factories were extraordinarily harsh and were frequently deprecated by the more enlightened observers. From the 1840s onwards, reporters noted the excessive exploitation of children (often as young as five) in the mills, and there is ample testimony to the effect of long hours and appalling conditions on the health of child, adolescent and women workers.[41] Children and adolescents were permanently damaged by long hours (16 hours a day was common), heat, damp, and noise. Reeling, before it was mechanised, used children to wind the capstans, with well-known results: 'Allow a little girl to go to the mill for a couple of years and you will have an imbecile on your hands.'[42] Women suffered from a whole range of ailments, but the most severe were those which affected their reproductive functions.[43] Nonetheless, the constraints on them to continue working were evidently enormous. They would work until about to give birth and they would return to work as soon as possible after giving birth, sometimes carrying their baby with them.[44] Children were evidently a doubtful blessing: they might eventually grow into workers, but for a time they threatened to disrupt family organisation. This is presumably the reason for an increase in the average age of marriage for women. Marriage was likely to mean that less time could be spent in the mill. Equally women put off having children in order to continue with work. And on occasions they disposed of children rather than keep them: the number of *esposti* (abandoned babies) in the Alto Milanese increased in direct relation to the growth of the female labour-force in rural manufacturing.[45]

Appalling conditions – in no way unusual in a process of industrialisation – are not really the central issue here, however, except in as far as they testify to the level of desperation of peasant families. What is more significant is that female and child employment outside agriculture became the norm for peasant families in the region, and families grew to depend on the fruits of such labour.[46] The meagre wages earned in manufacturing provided an integration of income, helping to supplement a standard of living in agriculture which was below subsistence level. In this phase of contact between peasant families and diffused industry, therefore, the possibility of earnings from outside the agricultural sector represented the key to *survival on the land*, and to reproduction of the family. For much of the second half of the nineteenth century such earnings often made the difference between continued renewal of contract and eviction. Eviction frequently meant a definitive break with agriculture – with no obvious alternative immediately available; the rural population continued to rise more rapidly than did the population of the provincial centres, and pressure on the land increased accordingly. Evicted peasants might have difficulty in finding a new landowner to employ them; those who remained without land might be employed for brief periods as day labourers, but were considered the lowest of the low, and labouring, given that the peasant family usually met its own needs in terms of labour, was a very short-term prospect. Landless labourers usually ended up badly, as one report makes clear: 'The condition of these people is anything but prosperous, and when there is no work for them they have no resources at all, and are compelled to search for their subsistence outside their native villages, or they become vagabonds and beggars, or provide large contingents for emigration.'[47] Rural manufacturing saved many families from this kind of fate.

Peasant men may have despised factory work as something for women and children, but – over the years – they came to depend on it totally. In any case – male attitudes apart – 'classic' proletarianisation of the family, with both husband and wife working in rural industry and ignoring the land, was impossible to contemplate. Without a house and a piece of land, families could not hope to survive on wages the low level of which presupposed some other source of income. In this sense, agriculture and industry were *not alternatives* for the families of the region: they were complementary activities, and if either failed the consequences could be severe. People who failed to pay their debts would frequently be forced to leave the region – some going to Milan, but many emigrating to America rather than to nearby towns, a fact which reflected lack of alternative opportunities.[48]

2.4. Family Roles and Peasant Conservatism

One possibility open to workers was, of course, organisation and resistance. But – in the period before 1880 – this proved a difficult path to follow. During the 1860s some (male) workers had tried to form a 'society' in Lecco, as we have seen, but the response of the employers had been immediate and successful. Peasants were in a very weak position. They were clearly unable to use the fact of having two sources of income in order to play one side off against the other – that is, to combat either landowner or industrialist, secure in the knowledge that they were not sacrificing all their income. This was undoubtedly because of extreme poverty, and because the two incomes were integrative and complementary rather than alternative: loss of either income was likely to provoke disaster, both in terms of immediate hunger and of eventual eviction. In a region of high population density, competition between peasants rather than solidarity was the norm.[49]

Competition was undoubtedly one factor in producing 'docile' workers, but was certainly not the only one. Attitudes and mentalities within the family also played their part. As already made clear, survival and reproduction of the peasant family were achieved largely through non-agricultural introits.[50] Yet employment in manufacturing, if crucial to survival, was still subordinate within the family economy to employment in agriculture. This was demonstrated by the fact that, for a long period after the appearance of rural industries, women and children continued to desert the factories at times when their labour was needed on the farm (this constituted one of the limitations of an otherwise extraordinarily malleable workforce). Contact with manufacturing and with wage-earning did not threaten the continued existence of the peasant family by suggesting alternative patterns of life, therefore.[51] In general, quite the opposite appears to have been true. Industrial wages permitted survival and consolidation of the peasant family on traditional lines.[52]

From the point of view of roles within the family it is extremely significant that it was women and children who went to work in the factories and that husbands remained to work as farmers. Before the advent of large-scale rural manufacturing, additional, non-agricultural, income for the family would often have been provided by the male members. In the region above Milan – and particularly in the Varese area – there was a long tradition of seasonal migration to France and Switzerland, where men could find work as building labourers or as farm-hands for a few months. Women would stay at home and do what was necessary to look after the land.

The introduction of rural manufacturing on a diffused basis inverted the roles, with the women leaving the farm (for a period of the day or the week) and the men remaining to work in the fields. Women would, of course, continue to work on the land in the time that remained to them. This rather pointed up the fact that, after families became dependent for survival on local rural manufacturing, women could replace men to a large extent on the land, but the same was not true vice versa. Men were thus compelled to see themselves as peasants, while their wives might consider themselves peasant–workers. This had important consequences for mentalities. Men, remaining linked exclusively to the land and despising the factory work, which they saw as demeaning, inevitably retained the values of the peasant male. And given that families remained rigidly patriarchal, it was thus the outlook of the men – that is of the traditional farming side of the family rather than the industrial side – which continued to impose attitudes within the family. These tended to be conservative, deferential to external authority yet authoritarian within the family, individualistic in the usual peasant way, and – in this region – strongly Catholic. Inevitably the family would tend to reflect these values. Women and children handed over their wages to the head of the family and continued to play a subordinate role.[53]

Family hierarchy remained strong despite the diversification of activities, therefore: male peasant culture continued to dictate relations both within the family and outside it. While women might become politicised in the factory and attempt organisation on a collective basis, they received little or no help from the men. The men might fear the reaction of the landowner – who might well be the same person as the mill-owner, and if not, was certainly likely to be on good terms with him; but equally they feared an undermining of their authority within the household. Women were thus subjected to a dual exploitation; from the employer, who benefited from the subordinate position of women within the family, and from husbands, whose conservative political culture played into the hands of both landowner and industrialist. In fact, peasant–worker families never managed to organise any coherent, long-term, political expression until after the First World War.

2.5. A Social Form, A Pattern of Behaviour

Nonetheless, the experience of work in rural industries during the second half of the last century did have a lasting effect on peasant family strategies. The experience established *a pattern of behaviour* among peasant families which was to remain a decisive factor in the subsequent development of the region. Integration of income from outside agriculture became the major defence against eviction from house and land, and also a means of defending the family. Whereas total dependence on one source could be disastrous if that source disappeared, several incomes – backed up by subsistence farming – made the loss of any one income much less serious. This interweaving of activities within the family meant that each job was paid very little, because employers were aware that they were not the only supporters of the family; this was, indeed, the basis of low-cost rural manufacturing. Necessity pushed the various members of the family to accept a high level of exploitation, both in agriculture and in manufacturing, rather than risk loss of contact with the land.

During the last two decades of the last century, one episode in particular illustrated both the importance of the rural population for industry and of rural manufacturing for the peasant population. The introduction on a large scale after 1880 of the mechanical loom for silk-weaving, traditionally the carefully protected and relatively privileged task of skilled male workers in the town of Como, induced merchants to move production from the towns to factories in the countryside, and to begin to use unskilled female labour in the place of men. Weavers responded to this threat by forming a militant organisation, but, despite sporadic strikes (which further confirmed industrialists in their decision to leave Como), town workers could do little to meet the competition of the low-cost rural workforce. A formal agreement between industrialists and the weavers' organisation, which attempted to limit (to 6 per cent) the differential between urban and rural wage-rates, and thus protect the weavers from cheap competition, was rarely observed by employers, who exploited to the full the divisions between skilled male and unskilled women workers. Weavers complained that they could not compete with people who derived part of their income from the land, while they themselves had nothing to fall back on.[54] Unable to find alternative employment, many weavers faced destitution.[55]

Despite underlying social tensions, of which everyone was aware, the 'system', based on the complementarity of rural and industrial activity in peasant families, probably reached its highest definition during the early 1880s. At the time it seemed that there were few factors likely to disturb the continuation of the equilibrium, so profitable to landowners and industrialists. Necessity, a rigid distinction of roles within the peasant family, the continued dominance of conservative and paternal attitudes among the men – all worked to preserve a situation of immobility within the family and ensure social peace. And the grain rent guaranteed a static relationship – the same immobility – between sharecropper and proprietor, in as far as it prevented any form of innovation in agriculture. Disruption of this system of immobility could come from only a few directions. If technological change in industry were to require increasing numbers of skilled workers, peasants might cease to be a suitable workforce (but technological change – as in the case of weaving – usually worked in quite the opposite direction). Equally, an expansion in the kinds of non-agricultural employment available to peasants might make them less disposed to accept the very low wages which were the basis of the profitability of rural textile manufacturing. In the 1880s both possibilities seemed a long way off. Indeed, for the landowner-cum-industrialist, peasant labour must have seemed almost the perfect workforce, with the men of the peasant families tied to the land by the grain rent, and the women and girls forced to work in the mills.

Notes

1. See most obviously A. Young, *Travels during the years 1787, 1788, and 1789*, London 1794, which includes a long appreciation of Lombard agriculture.

2. The description of agricultural change given in the early part of this chapter relies mainly on S. Jacini, *La proprietà fondiaria e le popolazioni agricole in Lombardia*, Milan and Verona 1957; K. R. Greenfield, *Economics and Liberalism in the Risorgimento. A Study of Nationalism in Lombardy 1815–1848*, Baltimore 1934 (1965); M. Romani, *L'agricoltura in Lombardia dal periodo delle riforme al 1859*, Milan 1955, and, by the same author, *Un secolo di vita agricola in Lombardia (1861–1961)*, Milan 1963; and L. Cafagna, 'La "rivoluzione agraria" in Lombardia', in *Annali dell'Istituto Giangiacomo Feltrinelli*, vol. II 1959, now republished, together with other articles which also concern the silk industry in one way or another, in Cafagna, *Dualismo e sviluppo* .

3. Cafagna, *Dualismo e sviluppo*, pp. 31 ff.

4. On these changes see Romani, *L'agricoltura in Lombardia*, pp. 77 ff.

5. For the early development of domestic industries in the mountain areas of the region, see R. Merzario, *Il capitalismo nelle montagne: strategie famigliari nella prima fase di industrializzazione nel Comasco*, Bologna 1989.

6. Cafagna, *Dualismo e sviluppo*, p. 104.

7. C. Cattaneo, quoted in Greenfield, *Economics and Liberalism*, p. 43.

8. The principal buyers were Switzerland and the German states, Lyons, London (Spitalfields), and Vienna; see G. Frattini, *Storia e statistica delle industrie manifatturiere in Lombardia*, Milan 1856, p. 58. Also S. Angeli, *Proprietari, commercianti e filandieri a Milano nel primo ottocento*, Milan 1982.

9. In 1855 Frattini estimated that, as a result of the silk boom, 'the value of farms was almost immediately doubled and the territorial wealth [of Lombardy] increased by almost 100%'; quoted in Greenfield, *Economics and Liberalism*, p. 44.

10. On the debate which surrounded the question of how best to adapt Lombard agriculture to the changed circumstances provoked by the rise in silk prices, see Cafagna, *Dualismo e sviluppo*, pp. 94–108.

11. The definitions of the family are taken from M. Barbagli, *Sotto lo stesso tetto. Mutamenti della famiglia in Italia dal XV al XX secolo*, Bologna 1984, pp. 15–16. The term 'multiple family' is here used to indicate a family made up of at least two married units. These units were likely to be themselves extended, in the sense of including surviving parents and other dependants. The almost infinite variety of families is suggested by a comment of the 1880s, in which the writer

almost despairs of arriving at a definition of 'family'; 'the word family is extremely vague, in as far as a peasant family can be made up of husband and wife and two or three children, just as a family can also be a father with four or five married children with their adult offspring...'. See *Atti della Giunta Parlamentare per l'Inchiesta agraria e sulle condizioni della classe agricola*, Rome 1884, vol. VI, fasc. 2, Monografia del circondario di Como, p. 47 (hereafter *Inchiesta agraria*). For a detailed account of a very similar kind of peasant family structure see C. Poni, 'Family and podere in Emilia Romagna' in *Journal of Italian History*, 1, no. 2, 1978, now reproduced in extended form in ibid., *Fosse e cavedagne benedicon le campagne*, Bologna 1982, pp. 283 ff. More general information on peasant families in this period can be found in A. Manoukian, 'La famiglia dei contadini', in P. Melograni (ed.), *La famiglia italiana dall'Ottocento a oggi*, Rome–Bari 1988, pp. 3–34.

12. 'Each family is controlled by a *capo* or *reggitore*, who is usually 'the oldest member, and who looks after both the internal workings [of the family] and the relations with third parties, in particular the landowner. He looks after the money, and hands out the food – when necessary – to the oldest woman, called the *massaia*, who is in charge of the kitchen' *Inchiesta agraria*, Monografia del circondario di Lecco, p. 371. An almost identical picture, which speaks of 'four or five or more married couples [living] under the same roof and [recognising] the authority of a chief called the *reggitore*', can be found in Jacini, *La proprietà fondiaria*, p. 226.

13. For a detailed account of the mixed contract (*fitto misto a grano*) see Jacini, *La proprietà fondiaria*, pp. 226–246.

14. Ibid, p. 264, where it is noted that some *masseria* remain, but that these constitute the exception rather than the rule. See also Romani, *L'agricoltura in Lombardia*, pp. 85–93.

15. This remained the situation for most of the century, as is indicated by the communications to the *Inchiesta agraria*; 'Now in the mixed contract, because it is agreed that as rent the peasant must cultivate such a quality of corn that, in order to be safe, he is forced to sow two-thirds of his fields with this grain, the remaining one-third is sown to maize to provide indispensable food. In this way any rational rotation of crops is impracticable, nor is it possible to grow an adequate quantity of forage to feed animals which would give manure' *Inchiesta agraria*, Lecco, pp. 366–7.

16. Ibid. p. 374. Romani notes that pellagra tended to increase during the 1870s and 1880s as the agrarian crisis hit living conditions: *Un secolo di vita agricola*, pp. 47–50.

17. In the final weeks of raising the silkworms, peasants were often forced to abandon the house and sleep in the sheds, leaving all available space to the racks of developing worms. As one report put it, '... the worms kick people out of the best rooms'. The worms had to be

fed almost continuously, even during the night – a fact which further disturbed the family. All this took place, of course, at a time of the year when peasants were heavily involved in other farm work. Some small compensation, perhaps, was the fact that the silkworms required dry and stable conditions in which to grow; as a result, peasant housing improved considerably with the expansion of cultivation of silk. As Frattini wrote, 'With the general replacement of other fruit trees by the mulberry, and with the change – provoked by the raising of the silk worm – of the ramshackle hovels of the peasants into comfortable and well-ventilated houses, Lombardy ... has almost totally changed its appearance over the last thirty years': *Storia e statistica*, p. 59. Jacini noted the same phenomenon: '... the raising of the worms compels the proprietor, in his own interests, to provide the peasants with spacious, healthy, and comfortable housing', explaining that 'It is enough to leave a door or a window open for ten minutes at the wrong time, or be late with the distribution of the [mulberry] leaves, or fail for a few moments to regulate the temperature in the rooms in which the precious insects are developing, and the whole crop can be ruined': *Inchiesta agraria*, Relazione finale, p. 65. Also C. Beldam, *Raw Silk: a peasant industry in the Brianza*, London 1898, p. 7.

18. Jacini, *La proprietà fondiaria*, p. 226 ff.

19. See Greenfield, *Economics and Liberalism*, p. 55: 'As a consumers' market, the agricultural population of Lombardy was not constituted to produce active trading. Its masses were peasants whose standard of living was low and who provided themselves with almost all their own requirements. The commodities the peasant bought were salt, rice, flour-paste, and bacon; all the rest was the fruit of his own fields. He was his own blacksmith, cooper, shoemaker, and tailor and the family spun and wove its own clothing'.

20. 'The *reggitore* is the most conservative man in the world. He would undergo torture rather than change the traditional methods. ... In his hands agriculture may flourish, but it will always be stationary. Try to impose a novelty on him as a contractual obligation; rather than agree, he will gather together his family and – in tears – threaten to leave the land on which he was born': Jacini, *La proprietà fondiaria*, p. 214.

21. Romani, *L'agricoltura in Lombardia*, pp. 139–41.

22. Ibid., p. 86.

23. Greenfield, *Economics and Liberalism*, pp. 27–8.

24. *Inchiesta agraria*, Relazione finale (S. Jacini), p. 75.

25. Cafagna notes that the figure of the *pigionante* is 'universally described as desperate'; *Dualismo e sviluppo*, p. 96. Romani writes of the contrast between the wealth produced by silk and the poverty of the producers: 'Overshadowing all this is the tragic reality of the boundless misery of the peasants': *Un secolo di vita agricola*, p. 8.

26. On the early organisation of the silk industry in factories, see C. Poni, 'All'origine del sistema di fabbrica: tecnologia ed organizzazione produttiva dei mulini di seta nell'Italia settentrionale (sec. XVII–XVIII)', in *Rivista Storica Italiana*, III, 1976. For the early industrialisation of the Lecco region see M. V. Ballestrero and R. Levrero, *Genocidio perfetto. Industrializzazione e forza-lavoro nel Lecchese 1840–1870*, Milan 1979.

27. Jacini, *La proprietà fondiaria*, pp. 204–7.

28. Silk went through several processes before it was fit for weaving. These were, briefly, the *trattura* (treating), in which the cocoons were softened by steam and formed into a shapeless mass; the *incannatura* (winding), in which this mass of silk was unravelled and the threads fed on to a spool; and the *torcitura* (twisting), in which threads were twisted together in order to increase the strength of the yarn. The first two processes were initially domestic operations, but then followed the *torcitura* into the factory.

29. Merzario, *Il capitalismo nelle montagne*, pp. 93 ff.

30. The information on Lecco is given by Ballestrero and Levrero, *Genocidio perfetto*, p. 18 who utilise a Napoleonic census of 1808–09; Greenfield (*Economics and Liberalism*, p. 86) notes the existence of 26 large cotton-spinning mills, and two large silk-spinning mills near Milan in the 1840s.

31. Disease ruined the production of silk cocoons in the south of Italy as well, and forced the northern industries to become dependent on the import of worms and cocoons from the Far East in order to supplement local production. See Cafagna, *Dualismo e sviluppo*, p. 198.

32. Greenfield, *Economics and Liberalism*, p. 80.

33. Jacini, *La proprietà fondiaria*, p. 18.

34. V. Hunecke, *Classe operaia e rivoluzione industriale a Milano 1859–1892*, Bologna 1982, pp. 207–8.

35. Jacini, *La proprietà fondiaria*, p. 18.

36. On the general characteristics of rural labour at this time see – apart from works already cited – F. Della Peruta, *Democrazia e socialismo nel Risorgimento*, Rome 1973.

37. Romani, *Un secolo di vita agricola*, p. 7.

38. Ibid., p. 110.

39. Ministero di agricoltura industria e commercio (MAIC), *Atti del Comitato dell'Inchiesta industriale*, Rome-Florence 1873–4, Deposizioni scritte, vol. II, Trattura della seta, cat. 6.1, sons of I. A. Gnecchi.

40. Ibid., testimony of Pietro Gavazzi.

41. There is a considerable literature on factory conditions in Lombardy during the nineteenth century. See, in particular, S. Merli, *Proletariato di fabbrica e capitalismo industriale 1880–1900*. *Il caso italiano*, Florence 1972. Specifically on the silk industry and the region above Milan is the study of S. Bonomi, 'Intorno alle condizioni igieniche degli operai e in particolare delle operaie in seta nella provincia di Como', in *Annali universali di medicina*, 225, 1873; substantial references can be found in G. Sacchi, 'Sullo stato dei fanciulli occupati nelle manifatture', in *Annali universali di statistica*, LXXVIII, 1843; and in A. Errera, 'Inchiesta sulle condizioni degli operai nelle fabbriche', in *Archivio di statistica* 1879. Passages of these contemporary observers are reproduced in Ballestrero and Levrero, *Genocidio perfetto*. See also L. Osnaghi Dodi, 'Sfruttamento del lavoro nell'industria tessile comasca e prime esperienze di organizzazione operaia', in *Classe*, 5, 1972. One needs a medical dictionary to understand many of the ailments, but – in case there are any illusions about the nature of 'rural' industry – the most common appear to have been rickets, scrofula, tuberculosis, typhus, pneumonia and other respiratory disorders, dysentery, distortions of the spine, hernia, and (not exactly an ailment) premature death.

42. Sacchi, 'Sullo stato dei fanciulli'. The article contains a full and damning description of conditions of child labour in the factories.

43. Adolescent and young women suffered in particular from disorders of the blood (chlorosis and dyskrasia) and the menstrual cycle (amenorrhoea) which frequently caused miscarriages and still births.

44. Bonomi, 'Intorno alle condizioni igieniche', p. 17, n.1.

45. Ibid.

46. The extent to which this situation was generalised in some areas is stressed by Jacini: 'One can say that almost every family has someone among its members who is involved in some industry unconnected with the cultivation of land'. See *La proprietà fondiaria*, p. 256.

47. *Inchiesta agraria*, Lecco, p. 367; also Merli, *Proletariato di fabbrica*, p. 122.

48. Ibid., pp. 377–8.

49. Petty crime was rife and served to set peasant against peasant. Usually crimes involved the stealing of food crops and firewood from a neighbour, but sometimes such actions provoked more serious breaches of the peace: *Inchiesta agraria*: Lecco, pp. 359, 378; Como, p. 67.

50. The importance of non-agricultural imports was perhaps best expressed by Jacini, when he wrote that – if the silk worms were to fail and the factories to close – 'the misery which would ensue would be such that Ireland would never have seen the like' *Inchesta agraria*, Relazione finale, p. 56.

51. Noted with satisfaction by Bonomi, 'Intorno alle condizioni igieniche', p. 11: '... it is a great good fortune that the factory hasn't yet succeeded in distracting them [the women] from their obligations and that industrial interests haven't prevailed in such a way as to silence the most sacred instincts and sacrifice to this extent the social priorities'.

52. S. J. Woolf, *The Poor in Western Europe*, London 1986, p. 67.

53. On family relations see *Inchiesta agraria*, Como, p .78; Lecco p. 371.

54. A contemporary analysis of the situation provides a very clear picture of the way in which rural labour was used to undermine the position of the skilled weavers. 'In the countryside, the workers who have laid aside the hoe and the mattock in order to dedicate themselves to the noble art of silk are the first to experience reductions in the agreed wage-rates because the industrialist knows that these workers represent (except in a few commendable cases) an element which is more malleable, more deferential, more easily convinced that the agreed rates are really too high, that the difference of 6% is simply a clever manoeuvre of the town workers to take away work from those outside; and so on, with many more stories and insinuations designed to fill gradually the minds of country workers with distrust for town workers. ... the town worker, who has no resources other than those which industry can offer him, holds steady in demanding the agreed rates; but in return he is continually threatened with unemployment, both because of the extension of mechanical weaving and because of its migration to distant centres.' A Bari, *Sull'avvenire degli Operai Tessitori della Fabbricazione di Como*, Como 1890, pp. 12–13.

55. Some were temporarily saved from pauperism by the establishment in Como of the Pia Azienda Tessile, a charitable organisation which handed out work to weavers while subsidising their production through public donations. The brief life of the Pia Azienda is a testimony both to the inability of the organisers to recognise that the crisis of the handloom weavers was terminal and to the extent to which paternalistic relations continued to dominate within the town: A. Avogadro, *La Pia Azienda Tessile. I provvedimenti per gli operai disoccupati a Como*, Como 1891.

3
Agrarian Crisis and the End of Equilibrium 1890–1915

The 'specific' character of the equilibrium which was established in the Brianza in the second half of the last century is readily apparent. Silk was in many ways a unique product, in as far as it permitted immobility in agriculture at the same time as it encouraged industrial development. Equally it involved the rural population in both the agricultural and the industrial processes, creating the interweaving of activity which became typical of the poorer peasant families. This relationship was based in large part on the very high value attached to silk – a value which persuaded landowners to continue with outdated sharecropping contracts rather than moving to pure money rents (in which there would be no guarantee of continuing silk production). Silk 'froze' social and economic relations in the Brianza and Comasco; it produced peasant families who relied on integration of income from several sources in order to survive, on the rigid division of roles within the family, and on a very high level of family activity. Again, it needs to be emphasised that agricultural employment and industrial work were not alternatives. Families did not *choose* to become involved in both sectors; rural poverty *determined* that involvement, and the fact that industry came to them, rather than the opposite, made it possible. But – even in the absence of choice; probably precisely because of that absence – a pattern of behaviour was established in which families relied on the house and the land on the one hand, and on non-agricultural income on the other. Before the turn of the century, the only alternative to this pattern was emigration or destitution.

3.1. The Impact of Crisis

The agrarian crisis of the 1880s and the consequences of the tariff war with France[1] undoubtedly served to accentuate the precarious position of peasant families. Although peasants paid a fixed *quantity* of wheat under the grain rent (and not a fixed value of wheat – something which would have required them to attempt to increase production even further), they clearly felt the consequences of the fall in the demand for silk. What landowners lost in income from silk, they attempted to recoup in other ways. Many families left the land under this pressure. The records speak of large numbers of more-or-less destitute peasant families flocking to Milan from the surrounding hinterland during the mid- and late 1880s, although it is far from clear what could have attracted them. And it is notable that, as the crisis became more severe in Milan itself, the number of peasant immigrants fell correspondingly.[2] Whether migration to the towns served to some extent to relieve the pressure on the land, and therefore to improve slightly the condition of the peasants who remained, is difficult to ascertain, but it would appear unlikely; as in any crisis, some people might leave, but many would undoubtedly cling to the land for want of alternatives, and others might indeed return to the farm. What does seem clear is that it is from the time of the crisis – i.e. from the mid- and late 1880s – that there are signs of some slow erosion of the equilibrium between farm-work and the rural manufactures on which peasant families depended. The crisis – in particular the crisis of silk – possibly forced peasants to look for alternative forms of non-agricultural employment, with short-term consequences for the care of the land. Seasonal emigration – mostly male – increased once again in the 1890s – a sure sign that the equilibrium of farming and rural manufactures had temporarily broken down. When the men left, women would remain to divide their time between the silk mill, when possible, and the land. Peasant families certainly had to find some remedy to the disease which hit the mulberry trees in the region in the 1890s (*Diaspis pentagona*), and emigration to France or to Switzerland was one such expedient.[3]

A further indication of change came from the Comasco. In 1889, after brief local strikes, the Agrarian Defence League of the province of Como (the landowners' organisation) published a document in which it voiced complaints that peasants in certain areas of the province (significantly those nearest to Milan) were now so well-off as a result of earnings in non-agricultural activities that they were beginning to neglect the land.[4] The truth of the complaints seems doubtful – at least in the terms in which they were expressed by the agrarians. Given that the report was published at the height of the economic crisis in the region, allegations of peasant prosperity seem difficult to sustain. Even so, the landowners argued (in the same document) that peasant priorities were changing in a significant way:

> In that part of the *circondario* of Como which is to the west of the town
> ... the *masseria* no longer represents, as it did, the principal – if not the
> only – means of upkeep for the *massaro*. Rather, it is becoming an ever
> more convenient way of finding a cheap house, food, firewood and
> money from livestock for himself and his family, who in large part are
> employed elsewhere and in other activities.

For the landed proprietors, the causes of this were obvious.
Emigration was taking away some workers, while 'others, who
for farm or family reasons cannot move away permanently,
always manage to find immediate employment and reasonable
pay in the building works in Milan, or in the innumerable
workshops of the city and the surrounding territory, or else they
combine intermittent work on the land with some craft or
profession'.[5] Consequences of this situation were not only
neglect of agriculture, but also increased drunkenness among the
men, and – rather unaccountably, if the improvement in
conditions described by the proprietors was true – a reduced
disposition among peasants to feed themselves properly, with
the resulting rise in the incidence of malnutrition and disease in
the family.[6]

It seems unlikely that this situation of alleged prosperity was in
any way generalised in the region. Had it been, it would be
difficult to explain the increase in emigration towards Milan, or
further afield. It seems more useful to see the document as an
expression of fears (based on isolated cases) – in particular of the
fear of loss of control of the labour force. Here, the Defence
League undoubtedly put its finger on the point at which tensions
within the local system might arise. For decades agriculture and
industry had been able to use the same workforce because
peasants were compelled by poverty to work in both sectors.
Farming and silk production were compatible activities, and
employers had not been forced to compete for workers. On the
contrary, peasant workers had competed for employment. But if
peasants were to discover that better opportunities for
employment existed outside agriculture and rural manufactures,
they might either leave the land altogether or begin to neglect the
land and the raising of the silkworms – given that it was an
extremely inconvenient and time-consuming process – and thus
deprive proprietors of their most profitable crop. The existence of

genuine alternative occupations would threaten to release what was essentially a 'captive' workforce by permitting farmers to meet debts through cash earnings rather than through the production of the cocoons. Peasants would, at this point, begin to be able to *choose* – and, even if their position on the labour market remained weak, this would constitute a fundamental breach with the conditions they had been forced to accept for most of the century.

It was not until the turn of the century that there were indisputable indications that – in a few areas – the balance between employment in agriculture and rural manufacturing was changing in favour of the latter. Proprietors again began to make accusations that, in the areas nearest to Milan, peasant labour was increasingly turning its attention to manufacturing, and that this was depriving landowners of their workforce.[7] It would appear that it was proximity to Milan which provoked this situation, with the expansion of towns like Gallarate and Abbiategrasso under the impact of increasing industrialisation. But it is highly significant that proprietors were quick to add – naturally by way of complaint – that peasant families who were now dedicating more attention to industry, and were thus less committed to agriculture, had no intention of leaving the land.[8] On the contrary, the house and smallholding represented a solid guarantee against hard times and unemployment. Where this was so, it is clear that priorities within the family had changed radically. For decades, female employment in rural manufacturing had been endured in order to permit survival on the land; after the turn of the century, however, the agricultural aspects of the family economy were retained in order to permit safer access to employment in manufacturing. Landed proprietors also noted that – in a very important change – there were now men of peasant families (almost certainly sons) beginning to take jobs in industries other than textiles, attracted by the higher salaries these industries paid.[9] Some peasant families – only a few at this point – were clearly beginning to make choices and to exploit alternatives.

3.2 From Peasant–Worker to Worker–Peasant

These were the first clear signs of a change in the balance of the peasant–worker economy which was eventually to become generalised; but the transition was slow and very gradual, and the development of the process varied from zone to zone. As long as the corn rent remained the standard contract, the majority of peasants were subject to a kind of straightjacket which impeded any initiatives or improvements in agriculture and which cost the family a great deal in terms of labour and discomfort.

Where change took place before the First World War, it was usually because some proprietors had decided to introduce simple money rents and to abandon the corn rent. This occurred principally in the Alto Milanese in the zones nearest to Milan, and was clearly connected to the increasing monetarisation of relations in the urban and suburban context (and to a tendency of proprietors to prefer money rents to the supervision of production under the corn rent, something which took up time and energy, and distracted from their newer interests).[10] Where the money rent was granted, families were much freer to farm as they liked, to produce for the market, and to use wages earned in manufacturing to pay the rent for the land and the house. In other words, their freedom to take entrepreneurial decisions was greatly enhanced. The concession of the cash rent in a few cases was undoubtedly an important example and stimulus to the many who remained with the corn rent.[11]

Before the First World War such changes remained very much the exception rather than the rule. The distinguished agronomist Arrigo Serpieri, writing about the Alto Milanese in the first decade of the century, noted that those features which in the past had distinguished the rural–industrial population still pertained. He recognised the fears which many nurtured towards the social consequences of industrialisation, but was happy to be able to report that,

> ... the nature of the industries which are particularly developed in the Alto Milanese – textile industries in cotton and silk which employ women and children above all, some domestic industries, particularly furniture – has meant that the industrialisation of the population has occurred not so much through the formation of families who work exclusively in industry, not so much through the growth of a real industrial proletariat, but through the employment in industry of suitable elements of the peasant families – without destroying, at least to all appearances, the unity of these families. Industrial employment

is a complement of farming; wages earned in the first are an additional element which goes to square the accounts of peasant families.[12]

This constitutes a precise indication that the process of change was only just beginning, and that the classic pattern established by the corn rent, with men in the fields and women and girls in the rural industries still persisted, with there being little tendency towards out-and-out proletarianisation of the peasant families as the result of an exodus from the land.

In the same work, Serpieri also provides a very thorough analysis of the physiognomy of the peasant–worker family economy in this particular moment of transformation.[13] The analysis lends itself to further comment. Certain of the conclusions are unsurprising – large families with little land tended to be poor and to derive a high proportion of their income (up to 75 per cent at times) from work in industry. Relatively few members of these families remained to work on the land, while the majority found work elsewhere. It was only in this way that it was possible to maintain the equilibrium between producers and consumers. Conversely, on the larger plots – which were usually the more fertile – families were smaller, and the number of family members who went to work in industry was proportionately lower; correspondingly, the number who continued to work on the land (which still provided the greater proportion of income) was higher. Viewed in the light of Serpieri's observation that the tendency towards proletarianisation (in the strict sense of the abandoning of the land) was very limited, the above remarks are particularly illluminating both for what they reveal about family structures and about peasant family strategies. The inverse ratio between family size and the size of the plot of land suggests that large families were seen to be of benefit in particular to those who most needed the support of non-agricultural income. In other words – rather paradoxically – the more hands you could send to the factory, the greater was your chance of survival on the land. For this reason, increasing subdivision of the land after 1900 does not appear to have resulted in a flight from the land. Families adjusted their allocation of labour between sectors in order to take account of such factors.

These conclusions are supported by an examination of the way in which the whole of the area above Milan became involved in the process of industrialisation. Broadly speaking, the process proceeded in 'waves', emanating from Milan itself, with the less fertile lands in the area of each 'wave' subject to an increasing level of subdivision in the years before the war. As the process of subdivision accelerated, so families became more dependent on industrial employment. In the Varese, for example, families often retained little more than a vegetable garden. These were the families which began to depend almost exclusively on industrial employment, with both men and women going to the local factories and leaving the cultivation of the land to the old, or to moments of spare time in the evenings and on Sundays.[14] It is to be noted, however, that even families like these retained their contact with the land and the house, clearly perceiving the advantages of their position relative to that of workers who were forced to move to the towns or the big city. Such families were now very clearly more 'worker-peasant' than 'peasant–worker'.

While landed proprietors might complain that peasants were no longer as dedicated to the agricultural process as they had been, in reality both landowners and manufacturers had an interest in maintaining the figure of the worker–peasant. Landowners clearly feared an exodus from the land on the part of peasants attracted by the higher wages paid in the towns, and it would appear that their fears were justified by signs of the beginning of such a movement; in addition, in the areas of silk cultivation, proprietors were particularly fearful of losing their most valuable crop – the silk cocoons.[15] That peasant families succeeded in integrating their income from other sources was, for landowners, a fact which permitted the continued heavy exploitation of those who worked the land for them, but it was important for them that this integration should continue to be provided by women – rather than by the men who worked in the fields. Much the same argument was true for manufacturers. Peasant labour – women and children – remained relatively cheap for the reasons already outlined above, was very flexible, and was generally badly organised politically. It was clearly in the interests of silk industrialists to maintain a workforce which, if it presented a few disadvantages because of its contact with the agricultural cycle, was nonetheless extremely well adapted to the oscillations of demand for silk. Moreover, even if imported raw silk was increasingly used because of rising levels of production, the owners of the silk factories were well aware that, if peasants left the land, they risked losing a part of their precious raw material. This was a very good reason for accepting the occasional desertion of the factory on the part of female peasant workers. The concern of both sides was, therefore, to fix labour to the land and to prevent migration from the countryside. For paternalistic employers, urbanisation and proletarianisation were both evils to be avoided as long as was possible.[16]

Yet, given that it was poverty which forced peasants to continue to accept unfavourable agricultural contracts and low wages in industry, the growth of alternative forms of employment in industry in the decade before the First World War threatened to destroy employers' control of the workforce. Writing in 1911, Serpieri was forced to note that peasant labour involved in the raising of the cocoons was grossly underpaid (when a monetary value was attached to it) by the current standards of wages, and that the peasants themselves were becoming increasingly aware of the fact that they could earn more by doing other jobs.[17] Serpieri sensed the undermining of paternalism; landowners were urged to adjust their sights to the new conditions of the labour market, or risk the consequences. It was simply not possible to hope that the system would survive on the basis of peasant poverty: 'in all probability it will become ever more difficult in the future to rely on low-cost rural labour'.[18]

3.3 Family Mentalities and Resistance to Proletarianisation

It might seem from comments like this that the interweaving of farming and industrial work was a system of survival which was eventually bound to be superseded, as conditions improved. It would be logical to assume that, as peasants began very slowly to benefit from their pluriactivity, as appears to have happened after 1900, so they would lose interest in continued work on the land. There is some evidence to support such an assumption. After the turn of the century – as has been already outlined above – the balance in activity of some families began to change, with the result that these families earned a far greater proportion of their income from industry than from agriculture. This was so in particular in those areas which had immediate contact with the hinterland of Milan and Milan itself, where evidently there were ample opportunities for work in manufacturing, building, and services, and where wages were higher than those paid in the rural industries of the hill regions. Improvements in communications served to make this catchment area of Milan very extensive by the first decade of the century, permitting the growth of daily and weekly commuting from rural areas.[19] It is also evident that, immediately before the war, some families in these regions – particularly those who had won the money rent – were no longer operating a purely defensive strategy of survival, based largely on debt payment, but were now in a position to pay their rents without difficulty, and were beginning to accumulate money, generally on the basis of increased industrial earnings. The general improvement in conditions among certain families is a recurring comment of Serpieri. He also noted that capital accumulation, for peasants, was related to aspirations to independence, which, in the case of peasants, meant possession of land.

Accumulation of capital, monetarisation of relations, entry to the market were factors which promised a greater degree of autonomy for peasants but which at the same time threatened the previously rigid hierarchy of the peasant family. Families might well have broken up at this point; it might have been expected that industrial workers within the peasant family would have been less ready – reflecting an industrial mentality – to hand over their wages to the common fund; squabbles might occur more frequently about how the money was spent. Yet, even if this undoubtedly happened in some families, the passage of that nineteenth-century system, which aimed purely at survival, did not mark the passage of the social form which had supported that system – the multiple peasant family.

What we find is – certainly – an evolution of the attitudes and activities of the family; but the increasing importance of industrial activity among such families does not appear to have led to an exodus from the land. Indeed, tenacious attachment to the land, a refusal to abandon agriculture, the desire precisely to avoid being 'freed' from the farm – all this constitutes the remarkable feature of this process of transformation, a feature which distinguishes it from transformation in many other zones of Italy. Why did peasant families, for whom agriculture had for so long been synonymous with poverty, not abandon the land when other opportunities appeared? And why did peasant families stay together, despite centrifugal pressures? The answers are perhaps more complex than might appear at first sight, involving not only specific economic considerations, but also certain socio-cultural factors which exercised a heavy influence on families.

It is clear that the land did represent what the agrarians had claimed two decades before – the possibility of a cheap house, of vegetables, chickens, rabbits, firewood, and so on. Many of the enquiries carried out by the *Società umanitaria* in Milan in the first ten years of this century speak of the very bad living conditions of urban workers, of the chronic shortage of housing, and of the high prices.[20] Rents for farm property were notoriously low when compared with rooms in Milan. This was, by itself, a very great incentive to remain in the farmhouse; rural hardship was still preferable to urban poverty.

Yet a closer look at the evolution of the political culture of the families in the region over the previous decades provides more significant indications of why pluriactivity persisted and why agriculture remained the central focus for the majority of families. Indeed, the different experiences of families in different areas of the Brianza serve to indicate that a variety of influences could produce different political attitudes and family behaviour without at the same time undermining the practice of pluriactivity.

As will be clear by now, the central feature of family behaviour in these areas is that the family functioned as an economic unit; individuals did not act independently of their family and local communities were made up of broadly homogeneous and related families. This economic characteristic was reflected in political behaviour. Both collective protest – which was usually communitarian, rather than class-based[21] – and individualistic strategies were engaged in by families, not by individuals or groups of individuals divorced from their families. Even where individuals were prominent – for instance in a factory strike – their action usually had to be sanctioned by their families, as was the case in the strike of the Brianza silk-workers.[22]

In the nineteenth and early twentieth centuries family-related mobilisation was generally of a defensive nature, i.e. to defend the semi-independent status of peasant families against the threat of proletarianisation. The concrete ways in which families mobilised depended on the availability of external sources of income and on the division of labour between their members. In eastern Lombardy (Lecco *circondario*, provinces of Brescia and Bergamo) individualistic strategies revolved around the employment of women and children in the silk-mills, the acceptance of help and subsidies from the Church and the landowners, the systematic recourse to (minor) thefts of farm produce[23] and, failing all else, permanent emigration abroad. Collective action took the form of peasant strikes and revolts, usually short-lived and unorganised.

As was to be expected, in this context political–syndical associations were less prominent than charitable and mutual-aid ones. This was not simply because the Catholic-dominated areas were characterised by a weakly-polarised and predominantly agricultural society, relatively untouched by and well-protected from the effects of the capitalist market.[24] In reality, the silk-producing areas were highly industrial by Italian standards (in the province of Como, for example, the number of industrial workers was on a par with that of people engaged in agriculture as early as 1901), although industrial workers were mainly made up of women and children from peasant families. As we have seen, it was the poorer families (the *pigionanti*) who resorted to sending some of their members to work in the textile factories, a clear sign that these families were threatened by loss of status and a process of proletarianisation. Yet, paradoxically, the acceptance of dependent status by women and children was in fact a means by which the semi-independent status of the family as a unit was safeguarded, and even served to revive its hopes of acquiring, in an indefinite future, a fully independent status through the purchase of land. Thus society was weakly polarised not because the population was made up of a stable class of tranquil Catholic peasants, but because social (and political) polarisation was contained within the family unit and neutralised by it.

To the extent that both employers (landowners and textile industrialists) and employees (sharecroppers and textile workers) belonged to mixed-interest families and were equally concerned to preserve the mixed economy, the Catholic subculture succeeded in promoting class collaboration and in introducing a variant of the old paternalism typical of pre-industrial society. Catholic organisers developed a series of associations and initiatives directed at defending the existing structure of local society. Peasant–worker families participated in this culture primarily as recipients. Nevertheless, the traditional Catholic 'themes' of submission, resignation and obedience, as well as the myth of the land, also served the purpose of preserving family unity and cohesion, at a time when women were gaining access to an industrial wage and might be tempted to gain economic independence as well.[25]

In western Lombardy (Como and Varese *circondari*) the loss of status of tenant farmers and sharecroppers was more apparent. In this area, a factory-based textile industry did not provide sufficient demand for female and child labour to offset the effects of the agricultural crisis of the 1880s. Here, as has already been mentioned, individualistic strategies revolved around seasonal emigration to Switzerland, acquiring or renting a loom to work at home (an increasingly rare option given the mechanisation of silk-weaving in the last two decades of the century), and becoming part-time or full-time artisans. Collective action took the form of industrial strikes (in Switzerland as well as in local factories) and peasant struggles, usually more prolonged and better organised than in eastern Lombardy.

In these areas three factors worked to ensure that political culture remained predominantly socialist. In the first place, the families' loss of status was clearly perceived as such, because it brought greater and more painful internal changes, requiring the male members (including the head of the family) to find work off the land through emigration. Farming was left to women and children and often neglected; as men sought to maximise wages and to fight their exploitation at their place of work, they joined a trade union and embraced the class struggle. Secondly, trade-union practices and socialist ideas were soon imported from abroad by the seasonal emigrants – a fact which Catholic sources registered with dismay.[26] Thirdly, the towns of Como and Varese contained important communities of politically active, radical and anticlerical skilled artisans, themselves threatened by a loss of status as their activities became factory-based.

The political cultures of western and eastern Lombardy depended largely on the local families' own perception of their status, and this, in turn, depended on the gender and age of those who earned wages outside the agricultural sector. What is interesting, though, is that, when considered as functional units irrespective of who did what, both types of family had much in common. Both, in fact, combined dependent with semi-independent status among its members and had the potential for developing a strategy aimed at achieving upward social mobility by pooling incomes and resources. As we shall see, families in western Lombardy took longer to realise this potential because they tended to accentuate their dependent over their semi-independent status – exactly the opposite of what characterised families in eastern Lombardy.

The persistence of pluriactivity was not primarily a consequence of a conservative Catholic mentality which linked people to the land, therefore; even socialist areas continued to recognise its benefits. Indeed, in Varese, collective action and strikes were the means by which workers were able to protect their pluriactive status and avoid complete proletarianisation. Varese serves to show that different political cultures were compatible with pluriactivity, and that all should not be attributed to the influence of a submissive and paternalist Catholic culture.

For most people in the region, however, the desire to remain on the land undoubtedly reflected the fact that, before the First World War, industrial employment among peasant families remained predominantly female, and that, as a result, despite a gradual change in the balance of agricultural and industrial income, the prevalent attitudes within the family were likely to remain those of the male head of the household, whose outlook was still more a peasant's than a worker's. Even where sons of the family had begun to work in industry, their position was still not sufficiently strong within the family to suggest any alternative series of choices to those presented by the patriarch. For the older men, in fact, the monetarisation of relations and the possibility of limited capital accumulation from industrial earnings was unlikely to prompt any course of action other than the reinforcement, by a variety of means, of the agricultural side of the economy. This might mean increasing the number of animals, changing the type of crop grown, improving the irrigation; security of tenure provided by an adequate income from industry might in this way finally encourage improvement. Before the war it was unlikely to mean purchase of land; land prices remained extremely high and few large landowners were looking to sell. That land-purchase was the ultimate goal, however, is beyond doubt. The events of the years after the First

World War, which will be referred to in the next chapter, make this quite clear. Here it is important to stress that aspirations to land-purchase represented a family strategy of individual social improvement, which tended to run counter to any collectivist or solidaristic culture. The better conditions which resulted from industrial employment tended therefore to consolidate rather than undermine existing individualistic family attitudes, and to confirm rather than put in question peasant attachment to the land.

3.4 Peasants and Protoindustrialisation

The persistence of the peasant family household and the mixed economy is the striking feature of the Alto Milanese and the Brianza during these years. It provides an interesting contrast with other areas of northern Italy – for example, the area of Biella – where contact between rural industries and peasant families resulted in the proletarianisation of the families and the virtual disappearance of agriculture within the family economy.

In this respect, the example of the Brianza also permits certain comments on the theory of protoindustrialisation. This theory has been applied by Alain Dewerpe to the area of the pre-Alps for the period in question.[27] His conclusions suggest that the area should be considered an example of successful protoindustriali-sation, in the sense that the passage from peasant domestic production of manufactures, through initial contact with the factory, to the final stage of the domination of the peasant economy by the factory, with consequent proletarianisation, constitutes a classic example of this particular path to industrialisation. The application of this theory to the Brianza presents certain problems, however. The principal difficulty would appear to lie in the interpretation of the behaviour of the family. Protoindustrial families, according to the original proponents of the theory, worked as a unit and maintained a degree of independence from the merchant capitalist. The earnings derived from manufacturing were only a secondary factor in the family budget; as a result peasant families continued to live on traditional lines until the incompatibility of continued agricultural production and manufacturing forced them gradually to accept the logic of industrial labour and to abandon the land. The behaviour of peasant families in the Comasco clearly has certain similiarities with the features mentioned above, but important distictions need to be made. It is obvious, for instance, that in the Brianza the penetration of rural manufactures into the countryside essentially destroyed the productive unity of the family, producing two distinct roles within the family – that of the male peasant and the female factory-worker. From an economic point of view, it can be argued – as Dewerpe has done – that female labour was a contribution to a single budget, and should therefore be seen as part of a single, unified, family effort. From a cultural point of view, however, these rigidly distinct roles were antagonistic; they cohabited only because the male farmer was still able to exert his authority within the family and thus dominate conflicting experiences. It was his authority which determined that work in primary and secondary sectors did not become incompatible and thus compel the family to choose between one or other of the sectors. This was to be a crucial factor in ensuring the persistence of the traditional peasant land-orientated mentality during the initial, prolonged, phase of peasant contact with manufactures and thereafter.

It is no accident that Dewerpe's work finishes with the First World War, when the stage seems set for the total transfer of the rural population to industry and its transformation into an industrial proletariat. Yet it is the fact that this does not happen and that peasant families in the Brianza continue to value the land which contrasts with the expected pattern. Here the example of Biella is instructive in explaining the apparently anomalous behaviour of the Comasco. In the Biella region small proprietors and their families had for long been involved in wool manufacturing, first in the home, and then, after mechanisation, with the women moving to work in the factory. For a time, the men – skilled weavers – resisted the challenge of mechanised weaving and managed to continue work on their handlooms. Eventually, however, (around 1880) the competition became too strong and the men were also forced to enter the factory. At this point the family became effectively proletarianised.[28] The similarities with the Comasco are many; but the differences are crucial to an understanding of the resistance of the Comasco to proletarianisation. A fundamental difference lies in the importance which families were obliged to give to agriculture. In the Biellese small proprietors were dependent on their own income from weaving as well as on the wages which their wives brought home from the factory. As a result, agriculture declined in importance very rapidly. Once the male weaver was compelled to enter the factory there was no alternative for the family but to accept almost total dependence on industrial wages; there was clearly no way back to the mixed domestic economy based on farming and the handloom. Division of roles, always less strong in the region, had largely ceased to exist.

Brianza families experienced a different relationship with industry. The production of silk cocoons gave a greater importance to agriculture and the requirements of corn rents ensured that the men remained totally committed to farming. While families were undoubtedly dependent on industrial wages for survival, in most cases they were able to retain a significant contact with the land. Even if their conditions were frequently fairly desperate, men did not go to the mills; the men were not weavers, as in Biella, and local rural industries did not want unskilled male workers. The division of roles within the family was thus maintained and the mixed economy of the peasant-worker family confirmed; paradoxically, rural industry served to support both agricultural labour and agricultural mentalities.

A further factor which contributed to the Como family structure was the difference in status of small proprietor and sharecropper. In Piedmont, land was extremely fragmented because the Biella small proprietors had for long been in a position to divide land between their sons. As a result, when the crisis of handloom weaving became really severe in the 1880s, the weavers found themselves with almost nothing to fall back on.[29] Agriculture was no longer an alternative. The same crisis provoked a different response in the Brianza, as we have seen. Sharecroppers had never been in a position to divide their holdings; peasants could either stay on the land or leave it, but they could not begin a process of fragmentation. Consequently, even at the worst moments, the plot of land usually represented a source of foodstuffs and firewood sufficient to permit temporary survival until an additional income could be found.

Rather ironically, therefore, the Brianza sharecropper did not leave the land and enter the factory precisely because he did not own the land he worked; the Biella small proprietor entered the factory because he did own land, but not enough of it. When, after the turn of the century, conditions began to improve for

Como sharecroppers – largely because of industrial earnings and contractual changes – the agricultural component of family income still retained sufficient importance to convince the men of the families that independence in agriculture was a valid objective, thus ensuring that families would keep their agricultural tenancies. In this way, they avoided, at a crucial period of industrial development in the region, the fate which protoindustrial theory has in store for them – total subjection to industry and consequent proletarianisation.

Notes

1. Following the Italian decision to introduce protectionist tariffs on a wide range of goods in 1887, the French retaliated with a tariff against many Italian products. Silk was not directly affected by these measures, but the acceleration of the crisis provoked by the tariff war had the effect of further accentuating the recession. See C. Seton-Watson, *Italy from Liberalism to Fascism*, London 1969, pp. 131 ff. Prices for cocoons fell disastrously (in 1870 a kilo of fresh cocoons sold for L. 10; in 1894 for only L. 2), a fall which was naturally reflected in the valuation made by proprietors of peasant production; see G. Luzzatto, *L'economia italiana dal 1861 al 1894*, Turin 1968, p. 179.

2. Immigration to Milan fell considerably after 1890, as urban industries began to lay off workers and building stopped. It began to rise again only after 1895 – that is, in conjunction with the improved economic situation. See Merli, *Proletariato di fabbrica*, pp. 124–37; Hunecke, *Classe operaia e rivoluzione industriale*, pp. 143–48; A. De Maddalena, 'Rilievi sull'esperienza demografica ed economica milanese dal 1861 al 1915', in (various authors), *L'economia italiana dal 1861 al 1961*, Milan 1961, pp. 80–8; Romani, *Un secolo di vita agricola*, p. 135.

3. Workers also went to Bulgaria, Hungary, Romania, and even Syria. See *Annuario statistico della emigrazione italiana dal 1876 al 1925 con notizie sulla emigrazione negli anni 1869–1875*, Rome 1926, p. 47. For further comments on this emigration see R. Canetta, 'Aspetti di vita religiosa e sociale nel Basso Comasco alla fine dell'Ottocento', in *Bollettino dell'Archivio per la storia del Movimento sociale cattolico in Italia*, XI, 1976, 1, pp. 13–17.

4. *Memoria del Comitato Provinciale Comasco della Lega di Difesa Agraria sull'attuale agitazione dei contadini nell'Alto Comasco*, Como 1889. The document begins with the uncompromising affirmation, 'In the present agricultural conflicts the right is entirely on the side of the proprietors'.

5. Ibid., pp. 3–4.

6. 'It is true that the day-to-day food has not improved at the same rate

as the rest [of living conditions], but the blame for this really lies with the lack of imagination and the rough habits of the *massaia* who cooks it and the family which eats it, or with the egoism of the men who, all too often, go off to drink at the tavern, or with the incredible avarice of some of the *reggitori* who hate healthy and appetizing foods because they empty the larder;' ibid., p. 6.

7. See MAIC, *Catasto agrario del regno d'Italia, II, compartimento di Lombardia*, Rome 1913, pp. 34–35: 'the land tends to become an appendix to the house'.

8. Ibid. See also E. Gruner, 'Studi sulle condizioni del contadino in Lombardia: abitazioni rurali, condizioni economiche di lavoro, alimentazione', in *Annuario della Istituzione Agraria Dott. A. Ponti*, VI, Milan 1906.

9. See S. Sioli Legnani, *L'alimentazione del contadino dell'Alto Milanese. Comeé e come dovrebbe essere*, Milano 1909, p. 4: 'But from the time when the enormous development realised by industry in recent years began to attract a large number of young countrymen to the workshops and factories...'. See also Canetta, 'Aspetti di vita religiosa', p. 18; and M. Cristofoli and M. Pozzobon, *I tessili milanesi. Le fabbriche, gli industriali, i lavoratori, il sindacato dall'Ottocento agli anni '30*, Milan 1981, p. 97.

10. On the transfer to money rents see L. Taverna, *I contratti colonici nell'Alto Milanese*, Milan 1909, p. 6 ff; A. Serpieri, *Il contratto agrario e le condizioni dei contadini nell'Alto Milanese*, Milan 1910, p. 256; MAIC, *Catasto agrario*, pp. 35–6; Istituto Nazionale di Economia Agraria (INEA), *Rapporti fra proprietà, impresa e mano d'opera nell' agricoltura italiana*, XIV, Lombardia (relatore G. Medici), Rome 1932, pp. 65–8; Romani, *Un secolo di vita agricola*, p. 140.

11. The demand for money rents was intimately linked to the extension of pluriactivity, given that money rents were usually paid *in advance* and required, therefore, that peasants had some cash in hand. This condition was clearly becoming generalised in the area immediately above Milan in the years before the war. See Taverna, *I contratti colonici*, p. 4: 'In areas like ours where industry and agriculture go hand in hand, where there are workers and farmers in every family and where the products of the soil do not constitute the only income, we ought to favour the money rent.'

12. Serpieri, *Il contratto agrario*, p. 43. Compare with the account in the *Catasto agrario*, published slightly later: 'On every hundred hectares of agricultural land there are about 400 inhabitants in the hills of the Brianza and over 500 in the Monza hills. This density, which is absolutely disproportionate to the resources of agriculture, can survive because in the rural families there are some members who, though they live in the farmhouse, are industrial workers, and others who, while they work on the land, have temporary jobs of some kind ... So, just as the proprietors gain their income from their professions and from industry as well as from the land, in the same way farming families

make their living from work in the factories and from carrying out some trade, as well as farming. You pass, almost without noticing, through a whole series of gradations, from the family which is still prevalently peasant, to be found in less industrialised zones and in the areas which are furthest from the principal centres, to the family which is prevalently 'worker' in the intensely industrialised regions and in proximity to the big centres. In the past the phenomenon was essentially a particular kind of co-ordination of agricultural and industrial work which seemed balanced and useful. On the one hand the intensity of silkworm production required by the proprietors meant that the farm supported enough labour to meet the maximum needs of the worms, while on the other the silk-mills ... provided work – even if badly paid – for the labour which was in excess of the normal needs of the farm. Following this, many other industries sprang up. It seemed advantageous to them to recruit workers among farming families because these, living in the farmhouse and using a lot of food grown on the land, were able to accept relatively low wages': MAIC, *Catasto agrario*, pp. 34–5.

13. Serpieri, *Il contratto agrario*, pp. 270–85; see also the analysis of this passage in Dewerpe, *L'industrie aux champs*, pp. 441 ff.

14. Serpieri, *Il contratto agrario*, p. 274.

15. Taverna, *I contratti colonici*, p. 6.

16. Ibid., p. 7, where the author warns proprietors that, 'at the present day, with industry taking the best minds and the strongest away from the fields', the concession of the money rent represents one of the best ways to avoid 'the curse of the depopulation of the countryside'.

17. 'My incontrovertible conclusions are these: that peasant labour employed in silkworm production is today, in the most common contracts, very, very, badly paid when the general level of wages on the labour market is taken into account. ... In most cases the day's work of the peasant, when performed away from silkworm production, is much better paid than when it is taken up with the worms ... so that the peasants feel ever more strongly the need to go to work in other branches of activity and to leave the land': MAIC, *Atti della Commisione d'inchiesta per la industria bacologica e serica*, Rome 1910–11, IV, relatore A. Serpieri, p. 642.

18. Ibid., pp. 654–55; also Gruner, 'Studi sulle condizioni del contadino', p. 10.

19. 'Many are the young people who almost every Monday leave their homes to go to Milan or to other manufacturing centres to stay there the whole week ... ': Sioli Legnani, *L'alimentazione del contadino*, p. 4.

20. Romani, *Un secolo di vita agricola*, p. 159.

21. C. Trigilia, *Grandi partiti e piccole imprese: comunisti e democristiani nelle regioni a economia diffusa*, Bologna, 1986, p. 64.

22. A. Cento Bull, 'The Lombard silk workers in the nineteenth century: an industrial workforce in a rural setting', *The Italianist*, 7, 1987, pp. 104–9.

23. See Chapter 2, note 49.

24. Trigilia, *Grandi partiti*, pp. 108–24.

25. A. Cento Bull, 'Proto-industrialization, small-scale capital accumulation and diffused entrepreneurship. The case of the Brianza in Lombardy (1860–1950)', *Social History*, 14, 1989, 2, pp. 186–7.

26. See for example G. Bonomelli, *Tre mesi al di là delle Alpi*, Milan-Sesto S. Giovanni, 1914. Mons. Bonomelli was the founder, in 1900, of a Catholic institution for the relief of Italian emigrants. According to Trigilia (*Grandi partiti* pp. 123–4), Catholic relief work among emigrants is to be attributed to a sort of 'compensation' for the more emarginated social groups which the subculture could not adequately provide for. Bonomelli made it clear, however, that Catholic involvement in emigration stemmed at least in part from the need to counter the increasingly successful socialist propaganda among Italian workers in both France and Switzerland. In his book he pointed out that one of the dangers of leaving Italian workers abroad without practical and spiritual assistance was that the emigrants themselves would preach socialism when back in their native villages, thus upsetting class collaboration.

27. Dewerpe, *L'industrie aux champs*,

28. F. Ramella, *Terra e telai. Sistemi di parentela e manifattura nel Biellese dell'Ottocento*, Turin 1984, Chs. 6 and 7.

29. Ibid., pp. 242 ff.

4
Peasants and Entrepreneurship: The First World War and Fascism

4.1. The War as Watershed

As in so many areas of Europe, the First World War provoked changes in Italy on a scale which is difficult to exaggerate. War requirements led to a vast expansion of the industrial apparatus of the country, and for the first time in the nation's short history, large sections of the Italian population, both military and civilian, were mobilised and put on a war footing.[1] Inevitably the strain was felt particularly in the north, in the cities of the industrial triangle, and in the war zones established on the Italo-Austrian borders. Workers were drafted into the factories and absolute priority was given to military production. Men of military age – those born between 1875 and 1899 – were, of course, likely to be sent to the front. This was particularly the case for peasants; in fact, between 60 per cent and 70 per cent of the regular soldiers came from peasant backgrounds – something reflected in the statistic that of the 600,000 Italians who died in the war, more than 60 per cent were of peasant origin; 64 per cent of the orphans of the war were children of agricultural workers.[2]

The effects of the war in the silk-producing regions above Milan were dramatic, even if they would not be fully apparent until the conflict was over. The slow transition of the kind noted by Serpieri for the decade preceding the war was subject to a violent interruption. Men were called up and left for the trenches; women were compelled to increase the level of industrial work (often in non-textile jobs) while attempting to keep the farm going in the time that was left to them.[3] Such changes in the pattern of existence were undoubtedly seen at the time as exceptional responses to exceptional circumstances, and were likely to be accompanied by the assumption that things would return to normal after the war. But it can be argued – and we shall return to this theme at the end of this Chapter – that in reality the war represented a watershed – an 'historic breach' – with the past for many peasant families, effectively ending a century-long relationship of subservience and dependency. At the same time, however, it is also important to stress that the fracture was not total: in a way it is continuity within the family – despite profound changes around it – which constitutes the 'specific' feature of this Italian mode of transition.

Demand for silk increased greatly during the war. Although the traditional markets in Austria and Germany were blocked, trade with France continued and exports to London grew considerably.[4] Silk had military uses (particularly in the production of aircraft, and of parachutes) which made it an important product within the priorities of the Industrial Mobilisation.[5] Even if imported raw silk had assumed ever greater significance after 1890, local cocoons were nonetheless at a premium and prices rose sharply. Yet peasant families were rarely in a position to take full advantage of this situation. With the more able men away at the front, an increase in the production of the cocoons was difficult, given the demands already made on other members of the family, and, in fact, production fell.[6] Even so, the increased value of the crop did prove of benefit to the peasants. As before the war and as determined by wartime requisitions, peasants continued to hand over the whole of the production to the proprietor; but the part which was assigned to them under the sharecropping contract was greatly revalued and assumed a new significance in the annual bookkeeping operation which took place between peasant and proprietor.

The revaluation of the silk production occurred in a context which was already at least partially favourable to the peasant families. Although conditions were undoubtedly harsh during the war, with women having to work very long hours in the factories and on the land, and with food shortages and requisitions making life difficult, certain underlying trends undoubtedly worked to their advantage. Contracts and rents were blocked at 1914 levels, with the promise that they would be prorogued at that level until the year following the end of the conflict.[7] This increased security, but meant little in financial terms to the peasant who still paid in kind. It did serve, however, to underline the advantages of the cash rent for those peasants who had already obtained it. These were able to take advantage of soaring agricultural prices while continuing to enjoy blocked rents. It seems likely that even those peasants still tied to the grain rent would have benefited in some way from black-market sales to the towns in moments of acute shortage.

Peasant women were, of course, in great demand as industrial workers. Reports on the silk industry provided by the Bollettino dell'Ufficio del Lavoro for both 1916 and 1917 speak of a heavy request for silk which could be satisfied only by continuous operation of the factories and by the repeated recourse to overtime. 'In all the factories work has gone on to the maximum in order to overcome the shortage of male and female labour, the first due to the call-up and the second to the substitution of men [by women] in other industries and in agricultural work. In many workshops, because of the heavy commitments, 10% overtime has been introduced ...'.[8] A result of this shortage was that employers were forced to pay more for their labour. Workers – almost entirely women (men constituted only 4.9 per cent of the silk-workers in the region in 1916) – were able to make repeated demands for pay increases. Arguing that life was very difficult because of the absence of their menfolk, women resorted frequently to demonstrations and often provoked strikes. These were illegal, but whereas male strikers could be punished by being sent to the front, the authorities could do little about the women.[9] In the end they were almost always bound to concede, rather than risk further loss of production. Almost for the first time, therefore, women workers found themselves in a position of strength and were able to exploit that position. One employer's report was typical: '... workers have been given pay increases for the whole period of the war ...'.[10]

In the light of the high level of social protest seen in northern Italy during the war, it may seem unreasonable to argue that peasant families actually made savings during the conflict. The reports of prefects and other local officials make it clear that protest stemmed in part from difficult living conditions produced by the war. Nonetheless, deposits in rural *casse di risparmio* (savings banks), the traditional refuge of peasant savings, did rise during the war, suggesting that problems may have been caused more by poor distribution and lack of supply than by inability to purchase.[11] It has to be remembered that families received subsidies from the government if they had male members away from home, and many families would have more than one person in the army.

In one way and another, therefore, capital accumulation may well have continued during the conflict, with consequences which will be examined in a later section of this Chapter. What does seem certain is that the war saw several fundamental changes in the circumstances of most peasant families. Increased wages for industrial work, blocked rents, the increased valuation given to the cocoons and to other agricultural produce – all served to permit families to wipe out their debts with the proprietor.[12] The importance of this change has already been illustrated in the previous Chapter. But what had been the exception before the war now became the rule. Equally clear is the fact that the war produced a generally increased monetarisation of relations and a greater contact between peasants and the market. In some areas contracts signed in 1916 even permitted peasant families to employ occasional labour and to divide the costs with the proprietor in cases where family labour was insufficient. At this point peasants had even become (temporary) employers.[13]

As we shall see below, the post-war period witnessed the results of the changed peasant situation; improved peasant fortunes were combined with changes of mentality and wartime experiences of the men in such a way as to produce an explosive mixture of hope and discontent. Signs of this were already present during the conflict itself. Indeed, the changes in the economic position of the peasants assumed particular significance because they were accompanied by a great increase in the politicisation of the peasant workers. Whereas in the decades before the war landowners and industrialists had been able to deal fairly effectively with the frequent 'agitations' through the mechanisms of the labour market, the war created both a situation of labour shortage *and* harsh conditions within the factory. This was a combination which inevitably proved dangerous, and much of the very severe legislation of the Industrial Mobilisation was directed at this threat. Skilled male workers who were sent to the factories rather than to the front were subject to a series of regulations which equated them to soldiers and which made them liable to punishment by military tribunals for even minor offences. So severe were the penalties that employers would often prefer to avoid denouncing workers to the military for fear of losing yet another worker.[14]

Tensions in the region evidently reached new heights during the war. Prefects' reports indicate that – from 1916, but more intensely from 1917 – the level of protest had become a serious source of concern. In almost all cases the authorities recounted that it was the women who took the initiative, often inciting the men to abandon work. This was the normal pattern for the war: women were not subject to the harsh regime of the Industrial Mobilisation and could afford to risk more. Usually women would stop work in protest against working conditions and the high cost of living; but these complaints would be associated with others – particularly with the complaint that military authorities had refused to concede leave to husbands in order to permit them to help with the harvest.[15]

Prefects generally denied that these were the real causes of the strikes and demonstrations – partly because they knew that there was little that could be done about them. But – interestingly for a region generally politically Catholic and relatively conservative – they chose to emphasise the political nature of the disturbances. In report after report, these were blamed on 'inflamers of protest' who were exploiting the fact that the war had gone on too long, that there was no prospect of peace, and that women feared that they would never see their husbands and sons again. Who these 'rabble-rousers' were was never made clear. Sometimes the blame was placed on soldiers on leave, who painted lurid pictures of the horrors of the front, or on letters from the trenches which, although censored, evidently managed to get some information through (a short message under the stamp appears to have been a common method). But the authorities had difficulty in identifying the culprits more precisely, as is indicated by the brief, but rather comprehensive, list of possible suspects provided by one prefect ('men, women, priests, clericals, socialists, anarchists, etc.').[16] What was clear to the local officials was that the scope of the demonstrations was essentially revolutionary. The women argued during their protests that, if they stopped production of war materials, the war would come to an end.

On the 8th of May, evidently following agreements already made with the organisers of demonstrations in the province of Milan, the revolutionary and anti-war movement in Lecco began. When the word was given, more than 150 of the women workers of the government factory belonging to Badoni refused to clock on, arguing as a pretext that the cost of living was too high, but in reality because they wanted to generate a demonstration against the war and visit other industrial sites to stop work there as well, saying that if war production was reduced the war would end ...

The strike extended to all the other factories of Lecco and the surrounding communes, so that on that day there was a general strike in industry.[17] Accusations directed at 'the class that wanted the war' were common, as was the belief – as reported by the prefect – that 'without a revolution at home, the war would never finish'.[18]

Such militancy was not reproduced immediately or on the same terms after the end of the war. Demobilisation during 1919 brought the men back to the families with very mixed attitudes. Many – the ordinary soldiers – had been radicalised by the war and had had their eyes opened to new possibilities. The promise of the land to the soldiers – made by the government in 1916 – was only one of these prospects.[19] At the same time, their attitudes towards family hierarchies had probably changed very little. The political challenge which women had presented during the war – a challenge which expressed a solidaristic culture very different from that of the men – was once again subjected to male control and to male values. Women, who might have been tempted by higher salaries to leave the land and become full-time industrial workers in industrial families, were restrained by the still predominantly 'agricultural' attitudes of the men. This conflict within the family, already present for several decades, was not resolved by the war. Indeed, it may have been exacerbated by it. In the short term, however, male and female radicalisation was able to find a focus in the fight for an end to the situation of agricultural dependency.

Demands for change in the immediate post-war period came together around one main objective. This was the revision of contracts in the direction of the realisation of the cash rent and the final abandoning of the mixed contract. Rapid inflation during the war and rising agricultural prices had underlined the difference for the peasant between grain rents and money rents. Inflation had risen much more sharply than money rents, which had been blocked at 1914 levels, and only the peasant who paid in cash was able to take full advantage of the rise in agricultural prices. Sharecroppers, still producing grain and cocoons to hand over to the proprietor, saw no comparable advantage. The contrast must have been very evident, given that a relatively small number of peasants had already won the cash rent in the years before the beginning of the war. And already in the course of the year – during 1917 and 1918 – many other peasants in the neighbouring regions above Milan had begun large-scale demonstrations in order to gain the right to pay rents in cash.

4.2. Postwar Independence: Family and Freedom

Peasants in the Como region were able to build on the precedents of these years. In 1919, they were certainly in the mood to do so, and the struggle for the revision of contracts produced a high level of political activity. In contrast with the past, for the first time most peasants in the region were no longer conditioned by debt. This apparently small change in fact represented a massive alteration in social relations. It gave peasants a freedom of action in respect of the landowners which they had never enjoyed before. This freedom was also reflected in a much greater disposition to take part in collective action; evidently fewer financial problems reduced the level of competition and distrust among peasants. As a consequence, provincial socialists, who had achieved little before the war, found themselves much reinforced; they were able to point to the success they had had in the towns, where workers had achieved wage increases through organisation and solidarity.[20] Peasants were encouraged to refuse to take silkworm eggs from the proprietors and to take them from the socialist union instead, in order to reduce peasant dependency on the proprietors.[21] Catholic unions, who remained the dominant political force in the region, also joined the fight for the realisation of money rents. In this way the strength of peasant protest was felt for the first time right across the region.

The pressure was felt in different ways in different areas and reflected the economic structure and the political culture of these areas. Mass mobilisation in Catholic-dominated zones (in Venetia as well as eastern Lombardy) differed greatly in scope – though not in form – from that which characterised the countryside of the lower Po Valley. In this latter region the mobilisation of proletarianised groups – the braccianti or landless labourers – was accompanied by a similar movement among a semi-independent stratum (small tenant farmers, sharecroppers) who wanted to buy land. The analysis of the different dynamics of the mobilisation of landless labourers and sharecroppers has illustrated the fact that in the Po Valley fascism made inroads among the upwardly-mobile groups precisely because the socialists were committed to collectivisation of the land. Sharecroppers flocked to the fascist movement in order to defend themselves from the collectivising pressures of the socialist landless labourers.[22] In the Comasco and Brianza, however, landless labourers were few and sharecroppers and tenant farmers did not really represent a vulnerable intermediate stratum; consequently they were not forced back into a defensive anti-socialist position. Unlike their counterparts in Emilia, therefore, they were not tempted to turn to fascism in order to realise their landowning aspirations.[23]

Nonetheless, the mobilisation of the intermediate groups, even where they did not join the fascists, could be equally destabilising. In the Catholic areas, in fact, the traditional élite was just as unresponsive to sharecroppers' ambitions as in the socialist areas, though for quite different reasons. Here upward social mobility did not threaten to break the alliance between proletarianised and semi-independent strata (such an alliance was already established through, and within, the pluriactive family); but it did antagonise employers. Individual social mobility had always been tolerated and even advocated by Catholic preachers, but collective upward mobility was seen as a threat both to social stability and to the mixed economy. The upwardly-mobile groups responded to this hostility, not by embracing fascism, seen to be the instrument of the employers, but by supporting the recently developed radical Catholic interests; they recognised that their aspirations could best be met by a new Catholic élite, representing the union movement and the left wing of the *Partito popolare*.

Unlike the socialists, who found it increasingly difficult to cater for both the virtually proletarianised and the semi-independent strata, the radical Catholics managed to retain their hold over both groups by promoting the sale of land to the peasants on the one hand (thus satisfying peasant–worker families) and by supporting some of the traditional socialist demands, aimed at (male) industrial workers (usually members of worker–peasant families), on the other. These included the eight-hour working day, the abolition of child labour, equal pay for both sexes on the basis of equal work, and family allowances – indicating that Catholic unions now accepted the principle of a living wage paid to the head of the family, something they had previously rejected because it had seemed contrary to the interests of pluriactive families, given that an improvement in male conditions was likely to have adverse effects on female labour. But now that mixed families were fighting to become self-sufficient in agriculture it was assumed that the importance of child and female labour outside farming – traditionally a thorn in the flesh of skilled male workers – would greatly diminish, particularly in textiles, where, thanks to rapid inflation, wages had fallen greatly in real terms compared to the pre-war period. It would seem that the new social order envisaged by the radical Catholics was made up of self-sufficient farmers and full-time and well-rewarded industrial workers. In either case the family would come to depend primarily on the activity of its male head.

In the eyes of the moderate and conservative Catholics, however, – those who represented local landowners and textile-industrialists – Catholic trade unions and the *popolari* were no better than the socialists and revolutionary propagandists of the Po Valley. After all, they argued, collective action was the tactic adopted by both. This deafness, indeed aversion, of the traditional Catholic élite towards the aspirations of the upwardly-mobile stratum brought about a division of political Catholicism into two opposing groups, clerico-moderatism and popularism.

Mass mobilisation and cultural changes after the First World War can be represented schematically as follows (Tables 4.1 and 4.2).

Table 4.1 The Role of the Subcultures before the First World War

Catholic Areas	Socialist Areas
Lombardy–Venetia	Emilia–Romagna
Catholic–Liberal Alliance	Socialist-Radical Alliance
in Local Government	in Local Government
Catholic Associations:	**Socialist Associations:**
Sharecroppers/Tenant Farmers	Landless Labourers
Country-based Factory Workers	Sharecropppers/Tenant Farmers
Tensions between employers and lower classes resolved through:	
Charity and relief work	Collective action and public works
Tensions between proletarian/semi-independent groups resolved through:	
Family unit	Local government mediation

Table 4.2 The Subcultures in Crisis after the First World War

Catholic Areas	Socialist Areas
Collective upward mobility of semi-independent strata causes:	
i. Antagonism between employers and semi-independent strata	Antagonism between proletarian and semi-independent strata
ii. Fascist alliance with employers	Fascist alliance with employers and semi-independent strata
iii. Break-up of Catholic culture (but lower classes stay united)	Resilience of Socialist Culture (but lower classes break up)

The above schemes do not take into account socialist culture in an area like western Lombardy, mainly because, as explained earlier, it represented an anomalous situation. Local seasonal emigrants were able to identify with a collectivist culture for a few months of the year, while for the rest of the time still participating in a traditional peasant culture. The proletarian culture had been brought back to their villages by them; but it had been superimposed upon a social structure which was still based on the pluriactive household. As households increasingly disposed of savings to invest or to spend – thanks to wage differentials between Switzerland and the emigrants' home villages – the peasants' perception of their social status changed and their loyalty to socialism withered.

Despite the hostility of the traditional élite, the demands for the revision of contracts met relatively little opposition when compared with other areas of northern Italy. In almost all of the northern hill belt above Milan the corn rent was abandoned between 1920 and 1921.[24] New contracts were no longer annual but for nine years, giving peasants greater security, and payment was now related to a percentage of the average *value* of grain and cocoons production over past years. Most importantly, peasants were no longer bound to produce those commodities, but could pay a money equivalent instead. Socialist and Catholic organisations agreed to broadly similar terms. Significantly, proprietors – realising that housing had become a central issue – now began to pay particular attention to the question of the rent for the house in which the family lived.[25]

The demand to be freed from the grain rent was in itself an indication of the evolution in the aspirations of the peasant family. This invites certain reflections on the objectives of peasant

families. To be free of the obligation to cultivate grain for the
padrone implied, certainly, a desire for greater autonomy in
farming, but also (not the same thing) a search for greater
freedom in the allocation of family time. This was especially so in
areas which were most involved in the cultivation of silk. Peasant
farmers had always disliked the rearing of worms because of the
discomfort it involved for the whole family during the final
phases of production ('the worms kick people out of the best
rooms'[26]) and the mulberry tree – as was well known – cast not
only the 'shadow of gold' for the proprietors, in the sense that the
leaves themselves were immensely lucrative, but also a shadow
which prevented the full development of the other crops of the
farmer. Even more important, perhaps, was the fact that peasants
had never really seen the results of the silk cycle. It was a cycle
which – for them – had been a means of survival, of payment of
rent and debt, rather than a source of accumulation. Its
implications were essentially those of a *static* situation in
agriculture, based on the need to keep the head above water. The
desire for money rents arose undoubtedly from the lure of
rapidly rising prices for agricultural produce, caused by the war;
but more fundamentally it represented a wish to enter the market
directly and to reallocate the resources of the family in ways
which were of more immediate and tangible benefit to the
family. This included changing the kind of crops grown, possibly
in the direction of more immediately marketable produce,
certainly in the sense of less corn and more produce of use to the
family. But it also meant greater freedom to dedicate family time
to work in industry, to contemplate the fact that certain members
of the family would work full-time in industry.[27] This was a very
different attitude – a much more *dynamic* attitude – from that
which had characterised the relationship between peasants and
the corn rent.

Peasant dynamism was expressed even more forcefully in
another respect, already anticipated above. Worker–peasant
aspirations frequently went much further than the conquest of
the money rent. The entire Alto Milanese, up to Como and Lecco,
was one the areas involved – for most of the 1920s – in the
phenomenon of land sales to the peasants. This phenomenon –
common to large areas of northern and central Italy – saw the
number of small proprietors increase dramatically, as large
landowners either lost interest in farming, transferring their

attentions entirely to the town, or sold up in face of peasant disturbances, fears of collectivisation, and increases in taxes on land.[28] Purchase of property was an ancient dream of the peasant, as is obvious, and the circumstances of the immediate post-war period seemed particularly propitious, with debts liquidated and agricultural prices rising steeply. Acquisition of land might appear to guarantee that long-awaited realisation of independence. But, if the intention of some peasant families was to return to independent farming as a full-time occupation, illusions were short-lived. Within a year or two of purchase, agricultural prices had fallen and prospects were bleak.[29] In fact, it seems likely that the original motivation was rarely that of a full-time return to farming – except for those few who managed to acquire fairly large properties. Land-purchase at the beginnings of the 1920s signified independence, but it was an independence which was to be utilised to exploit to the full the particular characteristics of the peasant family. This is suggested by the fact that, in most cases, the pieces of land in question were not adequate to support the people who lived on them. Family sizes fell between 1881 and 1921, but not to a great degree; and rural families remained significantly larger than those in the urban centres.[30] That famous balance between consumers and producers could be achieved only by recourse to extra-agricultural employment on an ever-increasing scale, and it was this that freedom from the corn rent and/or acquisition of land permitted. From the outset of the movement for the abolition of the grain rent, therefore, the land and the house were assumed to be viable only with the continuation of some element of family employment outside agriculture. Pluriactivity – which frequently implied continuing female employment in manufacturing or service industries – was, therefore, an assumed and integral feature of the family economy – even at the moment in which peasants fought for better contracts or began to purchase land.

Confirmation of this is provided by the fact that the size of plots of land tended to fall in direct relation to the proximity of industrial centres.[31] In other words, the greater the possibility of employing members of the family in manufacturing, the less important became agriculture. Many peasant–worker families were now predominantly worker–peasant families, with the shift in balance between the two sectors much more clearly defined.

The persistence of the pluriactive family may also have been confirmed and reinforced by the appearance of fascism. In reality, as we have seen, fascism had little to say to these regions. On the contrary, peasant families expressed either socialist or Catholic radicalism in the immediate post-war period, the new *Partito popolare* gaining considerable support in the struggles against landowners and industrialists.

Fascism achieved some limited success in the towns, but was chiefly the vehicle of employers and had little mass base.[32] Where violence was employed after 1921, it was usually through the agency of fascists brought in from Milan for the purpose.[33] Nonetheless, 1921 and 1922 did see attempts by employers to counter the mobilisation of the population and to recoup some of the concessions made during the first wave of disturbances. Lock-outs were common in industry, and fascist squads were often present at the factory gates.[34] Landowners also made attempts to redefine the contracts they had signed only a year earlier. Money rents were increased by 40 per cent in 1922.[35] Interestingly enough, however, there was little resistance to this counteroffensive on the part of peasants and industrial workers. The prefect explained why: of one lock-out he wrote, 'There is no danger of disturbances to public order because the majority of the workforce is composed of small farmers who at this time of the year go back to working in the fields.'[36] A similar comment was made about the sacking of 400 workers in one factory: 'the measure has been accepted with resignation because the majority of the workers are small landowners and peasants and at the moment they have work to do on the farm.'[37]

Such comments reflect a great reduction in the thrust of popular protest after the initial victories. It would seem that after a period of collective action, the old individualistic culture once again asserted itself. Pluriactivity evidently permitted families to absorb a counteroffensive without massive protest, partly because it was usually only one component of family income which was attacked. The generally worsening conditions of the twenties, which sprang from both political reaction and economic crisis, probably made families more dependent on the retention of a good spread of activities, where possible.[38] As all sources of income became more precarious, each was the more to be valued. To anticipate a theme which will be developed later, it might be said that the persistence of the pluriactive family through the inter-war period is in part to be attributed to the phase of economic stagnation which (after 1925) fascism represented; clear alternatives to pluriactivity were either absent or were unattractive.

A consequence of this was the return to moderate politics after the moment of radicalisation. Seen in perspective, one of the features of the post-war period in both western and eastern Lombardy would seem to be that local families, when moving from the defence of their semi-independent status to a positive search for social advancement, became more open to a variety of cultural influences, valuing each for the practical contribution it made to their overall strategy. In part this was undoubtedly a product of the war itself, which had destroyed many old certainties, but it was also a reflection of the fact that peasant families could now afford to raise their eyes from the day-to-day grind. The post-war period testifies in fact to the capacity of peasant families to take what was useful to them from contrasting political movements, combining for a brief period individual action and collective struggle. The peculiarity of this position is indicated by the way in which socialist and radical Catholic objectives were slightly 'perverted', or at any rate deprived of their original meaning, by the pluriactive family in order to fit in with its particular priorities.

This is best seen in the question of the eight-hour day for factory workers, a socialist objective which the Catholics of the PPI took up as well in order to attract the support of industrial workers. When the concession was made in 1920, the result in the region was that workers, rather than using their newly-won free time for leisure purposes or for rest, simply spent more time working the land or started up some other kind of secondary activity on an artisanal basis.[39] Thus the typical peasant practice of what was in effect self-exploitation produced – in worker – peasants – a strange distortion of one of the most significant conquests of the working class. Pluriactivity determined original interpretations of entrenched political positions.

In the long term this instrumental absorption and 're-elaboration' of cultural and political themes had important implications for the subcultures. In western Lombardy the predominant socialist culture came increasingly under attack during the fascist period, when new social policies, which aimed to destroy the collectivist culture and to reinforce family-related strategies, were introduced.[40] After the Second World War, socialism resurfaced on a much weaker basis, and was successfully replaced by political Catholicism, more on a pragmatic than on an ideological/religious basis. As we shall see, in eastern Lombardy Catholic culture survived almost unscathed, but only because it remained sensitive to the new needs and aspirations of local pluriactive families.

Families continued to rely on a variety of activities, therefore, even after the conquests made at the end of the war. The interweaving of agricultural and industrial activity remained a feature of the region. Female labour, and textiles, still played an important part in this mix; women and girls were still responsible for the greater part of silk production, for example.[41] But the most important change of the post-war period for family organisation – permitted by contractual changes or purchase of land – was the increase in the number of men from peasant families who moved to employment in manufacturing. This evidently corresponded in part to an increase in the range of alternatives available to men through the gradual industrialisation of the Milan region. Sometimes this move was thought to be temporary, with the intention of raising capital to improve land bought or to pay off debts incurred in land-purchase.[42] More often, however, certain men in the multiple family, now surplus to agricultural needs with the subdivision of land and the changes in cultivation, gave up work in agriculture and moved to industry full-time, while continuing to live with the family in the farmhouse.[43] This constituted a significant breach with the pre-war period, in as far as before the war pluriactivity had been present in the same person, so to speak (usually the woman), whereas with full-time male employment in manufacturing after the war gender roles within the family became less distinct.[44]

The entrance of men into manufacturing in much greater numbers than before the war had important consequences for the family. Male domination within the peasant family had always served to reinforce the static, rural, and conservative model of the family, precisely because it was the man who had no experience of the factory and of industrial relations. It was the transfer of male interests from agriculture to manufacturing which was to have the greatest influence in changing attitudes within the family, although this would require more than one generation. Male employment in manufacturing was, in fact, the crucial step in transforming the behavioural model established by the agriculture–silk cycle. This was a transformation of attitudes primarily, and not of structures. Complex families did not break up as a result of these changes; if anything, there would appear to have been some move towards the reconstitution of many multiple families.[45] Such families seem to have shown a surprising readiness to consider new alternatives after the breach with the conservative and patriarchal values of the past.

Accumulation of capital, pressure for changes of contract, and land-purchase were all expressions of an attitude which had been frustrated persistently by the silk cycle during the nineteenth century. This was a potential dynamism which had aimed at independence in agriculture.[46] Yet it is tempting to say that the eventual achievement of independence, or the achievement of much greater autonomy through the cash rent, after the First World War came at a point too late for the full realisation of the original ambitions. The land was too fragmented to support complex families, the wages paid in alternative manufacturing employment too high to be ignored.

Strikingly, however, families still resisted the temptation to leave the land and transfer to the towns definitively. As before the war, the worker-peasant model continued to have its *raisons d'être*. Rurally based families still had considerable economic advantages over their counterparts in the towns in the 1920s. The greatest benefit undoubtedly continued to be the possession or use of the house – usually large and able to accommodate the complex family.[47] In the case of rented housing, families paid little because rents for agricultural properties remained low; the contractual clause which required persons living in the house but not employed in agriculture to pay much higher rents (the existence of this clause was itself an indication of what was happening within peasant families) was impossible to enforce, since all inhabitants – at some point or other – lent a hand with the land or the animals.[48] In addition, the land which went with the house, however small, was clearly of benefit, providing basic needs of the family. Continued attachment to the land represented at the least a reduction of costs for the family. Minimising outgoings was as important as maximising receipts.

In reality, the 1920s saw a wide variation in the priorities of peasant–worker families, with some still giving pride of place to agriculture, while nonetheless relying on some element of industrial income; others possessed little more than a vegetable garden, and relied very heavily on industrial earnings. The general tendency, however, was to reduce the importance of agriculture. This was evident from the ever-increasing fragmentation of properties in the hill areas as the 1920s wore on – a fragmentation determined by the different requirements made of the land itself. Too much land could mean that agricultural and industrial employment would become incompatible. In passing, it may be noted that – in the old silk-producing areas, particularly to the west of Como – many peasants abandoned silk-production altogether, in part because it was a very high-risk cultivation for the independent peasant, while others who continued to produce did so with much less attention than before the war, with consequent low and uneconomic yields and poor quality.[49] The death of local raw-silk production had been proclaimed, in fact, the moment the corn rent had been abandoned. After the war most peasants had better things to do with their time.

Despite – or perhaps because of – increasing industrialisation, therefore, the social form and the pattern of pluriactivity which had developed during the first years of contact between peasants and rural manufactures persisted beyond that point to which it was strictly necessary for survival. The peasant family still functioned as an integrated economic unit; it continued to live on the land, even if the land was declining in relative importance, and it relied increasingly on extra-agricultural income. And, as we have seen, by the 1920s extra-agricultural income had become a source of accumulation for most families rather than a means of payment of debt and procurement of bare necessities. Only in one respect had the pattern of employment within the family changed. The proportion of males coming from peasant households who were employed in industry had risen sharply, indicating a breakdown of the original rigid division of roles within the peasant–worker family. In areas near to flourishing industry, as in the immediate hinterland of Milan, almost all components of the family worked in industry, leaving the land (usually a very small plot) to the attention of the elderly, or to spare-time work in the evenings and on Sundays.[50] In these circumstances, family roles became very much less hierarchical, with an increasing interchangeability of roles between components of the family.

Extensive wage-earning outside agriculture inevitably put the family under certain strains. There is evidence that salaried members of the family became increasingly reluctant to pass their wages to a central fund, preferring to keep money for themselves. Tastes changed through contact with manufacturing, and could be reflected in increasing divisions within the household.[51] This was sometimes a preparatory step to the break-up of the complex family itself. But in general it would appear that families withstood these tensions, preferring the guarantees offered by pooling at least some resources to the risks involved in separation, and recognising the essential connection between an improving standard of life and the large family. In this context it has to be remembered that – from 1927 on – economic crisis made it less easy to contemplate a secure future as a restricted nuclear family, separated from the multiple family.[52]

Population in agricultural regions continued to rise, therefore, even with the declining importance of agriculture. There was some tendency for population to grow more quickly in the areas immediately above Milan than in the Brianza and Comasco; but even in these last two areas population rose steadily and densities remained high – particularly among the rural population, where families were still larger than those in the towns.[53] The authorities were pleased to be able to report that there was little tendency to urbanisation in any case, and that the edicts of the fascist government, which forbade migration, were, therefore, irrelevant.[54]

The rural population, as it appeared by the mid-1920s, had very distinctive characteristics. Peasant–worker or worker– peasant families, according to where the balance of activity lay, had survived the war and the post-war revisions without losing their basic identity. The change in the post-war situation was that what had been essentially defensive strategies on the part of the families in the pre-war period now became slightly more self-confident and assertive strategies. Survival was no longer in question for the majority: a slow improvement of conditions and a certain level of capital accumulation had removed that problem. But social improvement was still based on the old pluriactive strategy of a high level of family activity, with members of the family now often more clearly defined as agricultural or industrial workers. The complex family, despite internal strains, remained an economic unit and functioned as an economic unit. Indeed, as we have seen, there was even a tendency for the recomposition of the complex family in the post-war period: as land became relatively less important for family income, it was no longer necessary to attempt any kind of balance between agricultural producers and consumers within the family.[55] The benefits of the situation were so evident that the family resisted temptations to abandon the land and the house, and to split into small nuclear groups. Even in the presence of political radicalism of one kind or another, the cultural attitudes of the families remained solidly linked to family individualism and to moderate politics – simply taking what was to its advantage from the different ideologies in play. The habits of the pluriactive family tended in any case to be more compatibile with the community-based ideas of provincial Catholicism (which in reality left the family more or less free to act as it pleased), and much less with more radical collectivist concepts (which in one way or another implied a loss of liberty of action for the family as a separate unit).

The family that emerged from the changes of the post-war period was anything but inflexible in its organisation and attitudes, therefore. Indeed, the salient feature of peasant emancipation in the post-war period was precisely that of an increased flexibility in a model which had initially been extremely rigid. As roles tended to change and hierarchies to become less decisive, opportunities for variations in family activities – whether male or female – became greater and the family became more adaptable to increased opportunity. What remains the significant feature of that adaptation, however, is that it took place within the general framework of pluriactivity, and therefore served to reinforce the persistence of the model.

4.3 The Decline of the Silk Industry

If the position of peasant–worker families had improved with the revolution of the war and the post-war period, times were nonetheless very hard in the later twenties and thirties. The revaluation of the lira in 1927 had the effect of revaluing debts as well as savings, and effectively put an end to the period of land-purchases.[56] To be a small landowner, dependent on agriculture, was in any case an increasingly less attractive proposition, given the growing divide between agricultural and industrial prices in the inter-war period.[57]

As it was, ever fewer families depended exclusively on agriculture. Large-scale division of holdings is evident in the statistics provided in the government-backed inquest on the development of small property holding in the post-war period, produced in the 1930s.[58] These suggested a dramatic increase in the number of proprietors for the whole of the area above Milan. For the Brianza and Comasco areas the increase – between 1919 and 1930 – was in the ratio of 100: 148 for the Brianza and 100: 155 for the Comasco (from 19,296 in 1919 to 28,618 in 1930, and from 12,823 to 19,792 for the same years).[59] That the individual properties were generally very small is indicated by the density of the population which owned the land. By 1930 there were 57 proprietors for every hundred hectares of land in the Brianza and 77 in the Comasco.[60] In general terms, as is obvious, the greater the density of owners, the smaller the individual plot; significantly also, it would appear that the smaller the individual plot, the greater the proximity to industry. These figures are supported by the more unreliable census data, which tend if anything to accentuate the phenomenon of the development of small landownership.[61]

The *Ufficio provinciale dell' economia di Como* reported in 1929 that fragmentation of the land had become excessive, and that agriculture was suffering as a result. The report throws some interesting light on the process.

> Almost everywhere there is an extreme diffusion of the small farm, with a relatively small number of estates directed by [large] proprietors and leaseholders and with a decided prevalence of small farmers and small leaseholders. This fragmentation of the land and of the produce has been provoked by the historical diffusion of industry through the zone and by the consequent attribution in many cases of a subsidiary and integrative character to the cultivation of the land in respect of the employment of one or more members of the family in industry. It has also been stimulated, particularly in recent years, by the easier solution it provides to the problem of the house ...

The *Ufficio* went as far as suggesting that measures should be taken to encourage the fusion of very small plots in order to make them viable as independent economic units once again.[62]

The phenomenon of fragmentation was linked, as the above report makes clear, to the declining importance of the land within family budgets. As more income derived from industry, so families who owned land could afford to divide land between sons and to turn their attentions in other directions, while those who leased land could permit themselves to take increasingly smaller plots. The more-or-less market-garden and the house attached to the land remained the key features in the equation. Even in the case of small leaseholders, money rents had confirmed the lack of interest of the proprietor in the running of the farm. The *Ufficio provinciale* spoke of 'very limited contacts between proprietor and farmer', attributing this to the fact that proprietors generally had other interests which took up all their time.[63] In these circumstances, peasant families were, of course, free to order their priorities very much as they wished. Here again individual family initiative could express itself more prominently.

Families were forced to look for new sources of income not only by diminishing returns from agriculture (largely a result of their own choices) but also by the accelerating crisis of the silk industry. Local production suffered during the twenties on several counts. Competition from China and Japan had increased considerably since the beginning of the century, and the Italian industry had undoubtedly suffered as a consequence of the disruptions of the war.[64] But many of the problems of the industry were linked to more immediate factors, relating to changing social relations in the silk-producing areas. Again, it was a report of the provincial authorities in Como which indicated the problems.

> The rearing of the worms, traditionally prized, and notably extended in the province, especially in Brianza, is in decline for reasons connected to the diffusion of industry and the fragmentation of properties into small family plots, worked directly by the families, often as a supplement to other – prevalently – industrial jobs; to the shortage of sharecroppers with sufficient financial means and technical knowledge; to the lack of interest shown by the landowner in the progress of the crop; and to other changes and cuts in the planting of the mulberry trees.
>
> Naturally other more general causes contribute to this decadence – such as the improved standard of living which reflects a general increase in income, the growing unavailability of rooms for rearing [the worms], the reduced preparedness for that particular task which is often in excess of normal work, the low return for the producer

when the accounts take into consideration the real cost of the days of labour, the decline in the market for cocoons, etc.[65]

Underlying these comments was the realisation that peasants – with their new-found independence – were reluctant to continue production of the raw silk, which tied them to a particular cycle and which was in any case unpleasant and time-consuming. In fact, those who continued to produce did so at levels which became increasingly less economic, falling well below the normal yields per ounce of the pre-war years.[66] Quality also suffered. Silk industrialists reported that women were not going to the mills because poor-quality cocoons were making their work more difficult. 'The aforementioned situation of difficulty [of maintaining standards] has reduced quantitatively and qualitatively the availability of the workers, who are attracted by other industries, even without the promise of higher wages, because work in the mill has become more unpleasant.'[67]

This in turn had direct effects on the quality of the thread produced. To be of use to modern machinery employed in the countries of exportation, the spun silk had to be of consistent quality, and this was difficult to obtain with a poor workforce. Spinning from the cocoons – even imported cocoons – required skilled and practised hands in order to produce a thread of equal weight and thickness – the main requisite of foreign weavers.[68] It was a persistent complaint of these weavers that the inconsistencies of silk produced in the Como region had an adverse effect on the quality of the finished product. Como found itself in competition with Japanese and American producers who could provide higher-quality goods because of greater technical progress. The antiquated structure of the industry in Como[69] meant that demand declined during the twenties, and – by the early 1930s, with the effects of revaluation now felt in exports – it was clear that much of the silk was being dumped abroad in order to realise much-needed foreign exchange.[70]

4.4. Peasants and Small Businesses: the Inter-War Experiment

The declining importance of agriculture in family budgets, best demonstrated by the accelerating pace of break-up of holdings, clearly corresponded to a development of peasant interest in other, industrial, activities. And the problems faced by the silk industry served to push peasants towards employment in other kinds of manufacturing. As has already been noted, the post-war period saw an increase in employment in manufacturing in general, and in particular an increase in male employment in manufacturing. In worker–peasant families the men were now likely to spend more time in industrial work than in looking after the land. Initially they were employed as dependent labour in a whole variety of jobs, most of them relatively unskilled, many of them reflecting the needs of an expanding metropolis like Milan and its hinterland. Improvements in transport now permitted fairly easy commuting throughout the region.

Industrial and population statistics for the inter-war period suggest, however, that – at least from the late twenties onwards – there was a significant change in this pattern. The censuses record a surprising increase in the number of firms in the region – from 11,177 in 1927 to 16,203 in 1939.[71] Further analysis reveals that most of these businesses were very small, employing from one to four people, and that they possessed very little capital equipment.[72] At first sight it would appear that a further transition had taken place; after moving from the status of peasant–worker to worker–peasant, families had now progressed to small independent entrepreneurship.

This is an interpretation which, unfortunately, requires a great deal of qualification. Had peasant families become successful entrepreneurs in the thirties, this book could more or less end here. In fact, things were not quite as straightforward as that. The statistics – obviously – need to be treated with some caution; but the phenomenon itself would appear to be unquestionable. The great increase in the number of small businesses was noted by the Como chamber of commerce (formally the *Ufficio provinciale dell' economia*), which evidently felt some slight embarrassment when forced to explain why small industries dominated. In a *Relazione* of 1930, the UPE testified to a vast network of very small industries spread across the whole of the territory of the province (with the exception of the mountain areas); these were industries characterised by the 'limited size of the single production plants' – a defect in the eyes of the UPE, which was corrected by the presence of a 'widely diffused traditional artisan class'. The report also spoke of the 'prevalent, even if [*sic*] diffused, industrialisation of the region' and noted that the expansion was not the result of Milanese speculation, 'given that the Como economy can count on a large quantity of capital and on a large number of its own businesses, often of healthy family formation'.[73] The businesses were particularly numerous in the areas of food production and catering, clothing, leather-work, woodwork (furniture), building, and, last but not least, metal and mechanical goods.[74]

What is less certain is the precise significance of this development, and here several considerations have to be taken into account.

The first is that the growth in the number of very small industries and businesses clearly coincides with the worsening economic climate of the late twenties. Revaluation of the lira and international recession provoked a general slow-down in the Italian economy, with consequent adverse effects on industrial employment. In the Alto Milanese and Comasco, where agriculture was declining in importance and where workers were transferring to industrial employment, the impact was obviously felt very severely. Many dependent workers were sacked, and those from rural areas were subject to particular discrimination by the fascist authorities and by the urban workforce itself. While the fascists attempted to protect the more politically dangerous urban workers from the effects of recession, they also played on urban resentments of commuters in order to divide the labour-force.[75] In these circumstances many former worker–peasants found themselves either unemployed or threatened with unemployment.

It would appear that the response to economic crisis on the part of many families was an adjustment of pluriactivity in which some – not necessarily all – members of the family moved from dependent employment to independent activity of some kind. This move was evidently not stimulated by increased demand: at a time of slump and stagnation market prospects were obviously not at all promising. Rather it was a defensive move which reflected the difficulties of the moment – increasing unemployment in manufacturing and poor working conditions and wages imposed by fascist unions. In a typically pluriactive response to crisis, families – unable to return to total dependence on agriculture, unable to enter the factory as dependent workers (as the Biella weavers had done fifty years before) – invented a new solution based on the continued functioning of the social form which had evolved over the decades, the pluriactive family.

It is important to note that economic recession was a key factor in this process. Had Italian industry continued to expand during the inter-war period, it seems unlikely that independent activity would have developed on such a scale. Continued expansion of large-scale manufacturing would almost inevitably have attracted more and more rural workers, producing in the end a substantial proletarianisation of the rural population. In this sense – as was suggested above – the stagnation of the inter-war years was probably an important factor in preserving the worker-peasant family from disintegration under the pressures of industrialisation. This serves to point up the fact that the processes described here are a product of the relationship between family development and external circumstances; as the Biella example shows, peasant families who achieved independence earlier and faced the challenge of industrialisation earlier responded in a very different manner. Usually they simply abandoned agriculture.

It is not the intention here to suggest that all the new manufacturing businesses registered in this period were linked to evolving worker-peasant families; clearly many were the product of the process of enrichment of a provincial bourgeoisie which had been going on for almost a hundred years. The silk industry had undoubtedly produced such a bourgeoisie, and the decline of the industry after the First World War may have encouraged them to turn their attentions to other activities. Equally, landowners who had sold up after the war had money to invest outside agriculture. Such people would find the local workforce particularly well adapted to their needs – cheap, flexible, and 'on the spot'.

Nor is it the intention to argue that peasants turned rapidly into entrepreneurs as their non-agricultural introits diminished. It obviously required more than a generation to move from work on the land to independent production in manufacturing. The older generation of peasants was evidently not directly involved in this transition, given that the traditional peasant mentality would tend to withdraw into increased dependence on agriculture in the face of recession.

Rather, the people who were of particular importance were the young adults – sons and sons-in-law, wives and daughters – but in particular the men. In the twenties, this was the generation which, following the war, found itself especially delicately balanced between agriculture and industry. Coming from rurally-based families, they, unlike their fathers, had their first experience of work in industry, although they continued to lend a hand when necessary on the land. Their financial contribution to the family was often fundamental, especially in the decisive years of the twenties. For instance, it was common for these figures to lend money to their parents in order to permit them to buy land or to pay off debts incurred in the purchase of land.[76] Such people had learned skills as dependent workers which could subsequently be put to use elsewhere. In this respect, an initial contact between worker-peasant families and non-textile industries was of fundamental importance.

Most important, workers from this generation, which had already seen the decline in the importance of agriculture, recognised that solutions to their problems could not come from a return to total reliance on the land. Their mentality was, therefore, prevalently industrial or commercial, but significantly different from that of totally urbanised colleagues, in as far as they were likely to retain many of the values based on the family, identifying in the first instance with the family rather than the industrial category to which they belonged and pursuing aims which were common to the family rather than to any political organisation. These were values which squared well with moderate Catholicism and tended to exclude adhesion either to the activism of fascism or to the collective solidarity of socialism. The family remained the fulcrum of loyalties; its members rejected allegiances which threatened to bring them into conflict with those loyalties.[77] But, as has already been suggested, the fact that *men* now expressed this mentality meant that such ideas tended to prevail within the family. It was now possible for families to unify around these ideas, thus reconciling the internal conflicts between peasant values and worker values which had been present before the First World War.

It was this generation – that is, the generation substantially in between a total commitment to either agriculture or industry – which was particularly hit by recession and economic stagnation. The reaction was, in a sense, predictable – but none the less significant for that. In the main, people simply survived as best they could – but *they did react*. There was little or no public relief to rely on for many rural families; in any case, people were not accustomed to expecting the State to help them. Survival depended on individual initiative, therefore.

The employment statistics for the period make it clear that many workers transferred to very marginal fallback occupations (these will be analysed in the next chapter).[78] People no longer totally employed in agriculture attempted to turn their hand to something else; workers expelled from industry after a brief experience of the factory did exactly the same. The rural population, caught in a moment of transition and without valid alternatives, was forced back on expedients, many of which reflected its past. Families attempted to exploit the one asset they had – abundant labour. The myriad small businesses clearly relied principally on this; capital was likely to be in short supply, given that the period of land-purchases had only just passed. As always, therefore, inputs of labour would be substituted for capital in an attempt to find a solution to recession. One solution which was not open was simply to move away. Fascist policies attempted to prevent both internal and external migration, although general economic circumstances were probably more effective in preventing the latter.

What is significant about this process, however, is that families did react to crisis by attempting to turn to independent activities. This was certainly a defensive reaction, only rarely linked to effective demand; but it does testify to a continuing effort on the part of the families to resort to multiple activities in order to keep their heads above water. Once again, the new activities did not usually replace existing sources of income which the family had managed to retain – they were more likely to be integrated with them. Initiatives in commerce or in manufacturing at first represented essentially a defensive strategy, therefore. Families would attempt to combine independent and dependent work where possible, in order not to be completely exposed to the risks of failure. Thus it is not unreasonable to postulate a multiple family in which there was income from the factory, income from private initiatives in small-scale manufacturing, trade or commerce, and food from the land which went with the house.

How significant in the long term was this apparent explosion of entrepreneurial activity? The issue of continuity between the fascist period and the second post-war period is complex and cannot be resolved simply through comparison of the censuses.

There was, after all, a World War between 1940 and 1945 and it is logical that, for this reason alone, many small businesses would be the first to fold in the face of the call-up, economic dislocation, and enemy occupation. That said, it remains true that small family businesses did form the backbone of regional industrialisation in the second post-war period, and we shall attempt to give a more comprehensive answer to the reasons for this in the next chapter. Here it is perhaps enough to underline the fact that former peasant families – now worker–peasant families – stayed together during the 1930s – indeed, were probably forced by the crisis to stay together – and continued to seek to exploit all economic opportunities open to them. The pluriactive model remained the key to survival. Significantly, however, in the inter-war period pluriactivity came to embrace self- and family employment in independent economic activity in commerce and manufacturing. This independent activity was characterised by the same features which had always typified families of this type, namely a very high level of labour input (the 'self-exploitation' of members of the family) for what was probably a very low return. In this respect, the expansion of family activity into manufacturing, commerce, and services followed a pattern which was not unlike the pattern followed by the early peasant-worker families in its contact with the factory. Initially the contact was enforced, defensive, and necessary for survival; only in a second phase did the family emerge in a position to express a more firmly entrepreneurial attitude. What interests us here – we repeat – is not so much the success or failure of the inter-war experiment, but the fact that it took place at all on terms which retained the family, the land, and manufacturing as central features.

4.5 Small Firm Formation and 'Historic Breaches' with the Past

This process of small-firm formation during the inter-war years was not unique to the area above Milan. But in other areas it may well have had a different significance. The case of Tuscany, for example, is apparently analogous. Giorgio Mori writes of the same kind of mushrooming of small and marginal activities in Tuscany after 1927 (i.e. with the onset of the crisis): he speaks of

... swarms of small and very small entrepreneurs who throw themselves with all the force of desperation into unlikely initiatives of very uncertain future (and the bankruptcy statistics serve to confirm this) and with a very high level of replacement. But their feverish, adventurous, incalculable commitment, the flashes of inventiveness which emerged here and there should not have been without consequences of some proportions.[79]

Even in Tuscany, therefore, it would seem that the entrepreneurship of the 1930s came to almost nothing. Giacomo Becattini, commenting on this passage of Mori, arrives at best at describing the phenomenon as a 'prerequisite' of the diffused industrialisation which would take place in the region in the 1950s and 1960s – a prerequisite which only the 'historic breach' of the Second World War would be able to build on.[80]

Leaving aside the question of when a prerequisite becomes a cause, the Tuscan phenomenon invites certain comparisons with upper Lombardy. In both cases small-firm formation followed economic crisis – something which is often seen in such circumstances. However, in the Tuscan case, the results were ephemeral and largely disappeared, through bankruptcies, even in the course of the 1930s. This was not precisely the case in Lombardy; small firms continued to increase in number throughout the 1930s and were hit – inevitably – by the war. This suggests important differences between the regions – differences which may illuminate the particular nature of the developments in Como.

It would seem important, for instance, to note that people expelled from agriculture in Tuscany had, on the whole, no long experience of factory work. There was nothing which corresponded to the silk industry in the region – something which in the Comasco had helped to form the social form of the pluriactive family during the previous century. The system of *mezzadria* linked the men to agriculture, and there was little possibility of men straddling activities between the primary and the secondary sector. Rural domestic industry, particularly that of the women *trecciaiole* (straw workers), may have supported the families of poor *mezzadri* for a time, but it seems to have contributed largely to the formation of an impoverished rural proletariat, which then lost its contact with the land.[81] The reworking of gender roles which was so important for the Lombard family rarely took place in Tuscany. It was likely, therefore, that small entrepreneurs in the Tuscan region were often making the jump from agriculture to industry without passing through the intermediate stage of the worker–peasant family, something which, in Lombardy, had served to amalgamate both agricultural and industrial interests. This might have consequences both for the level of commercial and manufacturing skills available to the would-be entrepreneur, and for the economic viability of a new enterprise. Pluriactive families in Lombardy always had fallback positions in the case of failure of one activity; Tuscan families who had attempted the total transfer from agriculture to manufacturing did not.

This is just another way of saying that the agricultural structure of the two regions was very different, and that agriculture had assumed a different significance for the families who lived in rural areas. Tuscany saw relatively little change in agricultural holding after the First World War. Only some 30,000 hectares changed hands, compared with 150,000 in Lombardy.[82] Fascism served to shore up the system of *mezzadria* for the inter-war period in the face of the considerable challenge that had been made to it. As a result there was no formation of a significant class of new small proprietors, and no subdivision of holdings as was witnessed in the Brianza. In Tuscany, men who remained in agriculture remained with a system of *mezzadria* which required all their attention and gave no room to the establishment of pluriactivity. There was no decline in the importance of agriculture within family budgets, as there was further north. It was this that determined that small firms in Tuscany had less possibility of survival than in Lombardy; small firms were not based on the rurally-based pluriactive family, but on people who, necessarily, had already left the land.

For Becattini the growth of diffused industrialisation in Tuscany is related to the 'historic breach' provided by the Second World War, which undermined traditional values and effectively signalled the final crisis of the system of *mezzadria*, thus freeing people for other activities.[83] Entrepreneurial abilities and aspirations were finally released and were able to exploit the qualities of low cost and flexibility offered by former-peasant labour in a moment of rapidly rising demand. Interestingly, sharecroppers no longer aspired to landownership: the need for heavy investment in agriculture (machines, fertilizers) made farming a difficult prospect for small family units.[84]

It does not seem an exaggeration to suggest that the same kind of historic breach was provided for Upper Lombardy by the First World War. As we have seen, the war marked the watershed between the enslavement of a large proportion of rural families to the silk cycle and the grain rent, and a much greater degree of autonomy and independence. Equally the war and the immediate post-war period made clear the end of paternalistic relations and ratified a new kind of moderate Catholicism which went well with family aspirations. These were fundamental breaches with the past, and placed peasant families in a position radically different from that of the Tuscan *mezzadro*. The small entrepreneurs of the Como and the Brianza started from very different bases during the late 1920s and 1930s, therefore; their relative lack of success is to be linked to the particular circumstances of the inter-war years – that is, more to market conditions, economic stagnation, and war, than to the inability of the social form of the worker-peasant family to extend itself in this way. The *offer* of certain qualities and characteristics was already present; what was missing in the 1930s was the *demand*.

Notes

1. On industrial and social mobilisation see Giovanna Procacci (ed.), *Stato e classe operaia in Italia durante la prima guerra mondiale*, Milan 1983; in particular id., 'La legislazione repressiva e la sua applicazione', and L. Tomassini, 'Mobilitazione industriale e classe operaia'.

2. See A. Serpieri, *La guerra e le classi rurali italiane*, Bari 1930, p. 42. The author notes that peasants constituted less than 50 per cent of the entire armed forces; their greater losses are indicative of the fact that they made up the bulk of the front-line troops.

3. See MAIC, *Bollettino dell'Ufficio del Lavoro*, 1916, IV trimestre, p. 91; ibid., 1917 II trimestre, p. 202; A. Molinari, *Contratti di lavoro e salari nelle aziende agricole dell'Alto e Basso Milanese*, Milan 1923, p. 13; Manoukian, 'La famiglia italiana', p. 23.

4. ACS, Ministero dell'Interno, Divisione Polizia Giudiziaria 1916–1918, b. 260, Sindacato Italiano Tessile and Federazione Comense del Lavoro to Prime Minister Boselli, 23 July 1916.

5. On the problems of the silk industry during the war see ACS, Ministero per le armi e munizioni, Comitato centrale di Mobilitazione industriale, b. 228.

6. National production fell from almost 47 million kg. of fresh cocoons in 1914 to less than 30 million kg. in 1918. See Istituto Centrale di Statistica, *Sommario di statistiche storiche italiane 1861–1955*, Rome 1958, p. 115.

7. Serpieri, *La guerra e le classi rurali*, pp. 131–6; Molinari, *Contratti di lavoro*, p. 13.

8. MAIC, *Bollettino dell'Ufficio del Lavoro*, 1916, IV trimestre, p. 91.

9. Giovanna Procacci, 'Dalla rassegnazione alla rivolta: osservazioni sul comportamento popolare in Italia negli anni della prima guerra mondiale', in *Ricerche storiche*, XIX, 1, 1989, pp. 81–2.

10. MAIC, *Bollettino dell'Ufficio del Lavoro*, 1916, IV trimestre, p. 91.

11. On increases in peasant savings see Serpieri, *La guerra e le classe rurali*, pp. 131–2; also Romani, *L'agricoltura in Lombardia*, p. 161.

12. Serpieri, *La guerra e le classi rurali*, pp. 134–8; Molinari, *Contratti di lavoro*, p. 36–7.

13. Molinari, *Contratti di lavoro*, p. 22.

14. Procacci, 'La legislazione repressiva', pp. 53–4.

15. Procacci, 'Dalla rassegnazione alla rivolta', pp. 78–9.

16. ACS, Ministero dell'Interno, Direzione Generale Pubblica Sicurezza, AGR, cat. A5G, Conflagrazione europea, b. 92, fasc. 207, 6 June 1917.

17. Ibid.

18. Ibid.

19. See A. Papa, 'Guerra e terra 1915–1918', in *Studi storici*, X, 1, 1969, pp. 3–45.

20. *La Brianza*, 26 April 1919.

21. Molinari, *Contratti di lavoro*, p. 26.

22. P. Corner, *Fascism in Ferrara 1915–25*, Oxford 1975, Ch. 7.

23. In the November 1919 elections in Monza, for example, the fascists polled 99 votes in a turn-out of 33,518 voters. See *La Brianza*, 19 November 1919.

24. *La Brianza*, 14 February 1920, which announces the abolition of the existing contracts.

25. Molinari, *Contratti di lavoro*, pp. 36–51.

26. MAIC, *Atti della Commissione d'inchiesta per la industria bacologica e serica*, Rome 1910–11, IV, *relatore* A. Serpieri, p. 651.

27. Molinari noted the close relationship between contact with industry and the desire for independence: 'Contact with industry means contact

with the spirit of class and of independence which encourages the peasant to struggle to obtain better returns and more flexible contracts ... In this way the mentality of the peasant changes, preparing the path for the money rent, which satisfies this desire for independence: *Contratti di lavoro*, p. 21.

28. On the phenomenon of peasant purchases of land in the post war period, see R. Rossi, *Inchiesta sulla piccola proprietà coltivatrice formatasi nel dopoguerra, Lombardia*, Rome 1931. This is part of the national study directed by G. Lorenzoni; see id., *Inchiesta sulla piccola proprietà coltivatrice formatasi nel dopoguerra. Relazione finale: l'ascesa del contadino italiano nel dopoguerra*, Roma 1938; also Molinari, *Contratti di lavoro*, pp. 4–5.

29. Molinari, *Contratti di lavoro*, pp. 60–5.

30. Rossi, *Inchiesta sulla piccola proprietà*, pp. 18–21.

31. See Istituto Nazionale di Economica Agraria, *Rapporti fra proprietà, impresa e mano d'opera nell'agricoltura italiana*, XIV, *Lombardia* (relatore Giuseppe Medici), Rome 1932, p.65: 'there is a close correlation everywhere between the average size of the farm, or of the plot, and the greater or lesser intensity of industrial development'; Molinari, *Contratti di lavoro*, p.10: 'the size of the holding is in function of, and regulated by, the extra-agricultural activities of the farm'; also noted in Rossi, *Inchiesta sulla piccola proprietà*, pp. 50–1.

32. *Il Lavoratore comasco*, 22 June 1921, where the socialists felt sufficiently confident to be able to observe that 'the fascism of Como is better than many others; it is less hydrophobic, less rabid, less bilious'.

33. ACS, Ministero dell'Interno, Direzione Generale Pubblica Sicurezza, AGR, 1921, b. 65, Sindacato Edile Como to Prime Minister Bonomi, 26 July 1921. The building workers complained that the carabinieri were partial and that, when they had difficulty in keeping order, 'they have the nerve to say explicitly that if we don't behave, they will call the Fascists. We are sure that the orders issued by Your Excellence are not these!'

34. ACS, ibid., 1922, b. 64, 12 April 1922.

35. Molinari, *Contratti di lavoro*, p. 61.

36. ACS, Ministero dell'Interno, Direzione Generale Pubblica Sicurezza, AGR, 1921, p. 65, 20 July 1921.

37. ACS, ibid., 4 June 1921.

38. On contractual changes during this period see, in general, G. Giorgetti, *Contadini e proprietari nell'Italia moderna. Rapporti di produzione e contratti agrari dal secolo XVI a oggi*, Turin 1974, Ch. 8; also A. Del Re, 'I patti agrari dell'Alto Milanese dalla restaurazione contrattuale fascista alla grande crisi', in (various authors), *Agricoltura e forze sociali in Lombardia nella crisi degli anni trenta*, Milan 1983.

39. This was, of course, not surprising for workers who had been accustomed to working 12–16 hours a day for generations.

40. See for example V. de Grazia, *The Culture of Consent. The Mass Organisation of Leisure in Fascist Italy*, Cambridge 1981.

41. In 1903 women had made up 66 per cent of all industrial workers in the province of Como. By 1927 they constituted only 45 per cent, but they still represented some 70 per cent of textile workers; MAIC, *Censimento industriale 1911*, vol. V, prospetto IV, Rome 1916; Ufficio provinciale dell'economia – Como, *Alcuni dati statistici sull'economia della provincia*, table V, Como 1929.

42. Rossi, *Inchiesta sulla piccola proprietà* p. 63; Rossi also notes the role of the Catholic banks in providing credit and other assistance to peasants who wanted to buy land.

43. Ibid., p. 42: 'the worker remained a farmer only in order to keep the house and to improve the family budget a little'.

44. P. Corner, 'Women and fascism. Changing family roles in the transition from an agricultural to an industrial society' in *European History Quarterly*, 1, 1993.

45. On the tendency towards a recomposition of the multiple family in these years see Barbagli, *Sotto lo stesso tetto*, pp.108–13.

46. Rare cases of peasant accumulation were noted in the *Inchiesta agraria* of 1882. 'As far as the peasants are concerned the great majority have only a very small amount of capital which is invested in one or two animals, but there are those in the countryside who, through some business side-line (the sale of animals or the like) accumulate a reasonable sum, which allows them to buy a small house and a few square yards of land.' The importance of extra-agricultural income is emphasised in a later observation: 'It has to be noted that the peasants who accumulate money are in general those who, either directly or through some member of the family, have earnings in commerce or in industry': *Inchiesta agraria*, Como, p. 58, p. 84.

47. Housing in the Milan area was in notoriously short supply after the First World War and government legislation on rents discouraged further building: Molinari, *Contratti di lavoro*, p. 58, where the author speaks of 'the enormous difficulty of finding living accommodation'; also Rossi, *Inchiesta sulla piccola proprietà*, pp. 42–45.

48. Rossi, *Inchiesta sulla piccola proprietà*, p. 44.

49. The difficulties which the silk industry encountered had been accurately predicted by Serpieri in 1911, when he had warned that the interests of peasants and proprietors were very different and that this difference would be reflected sooner or later in the neglect or abandonment of cocoon production: MAIC, *Atti della Commissione d'Inchiesta per la industria bacologica e serica*, pp. 653–5; also Molinari,

Contratti di lavoro, p. 62.

50. See Rossi, *Inchiesta sulla piccola proprietà,* p. 42.

51. Ibid., p. 19.

52. Barbagli, *Sotto lo stesso tetto,* pp. 100–8.

53. See Rossi, *Inchiesta sulla piccola proprietà,* pp. 18–20.

54. Ufficio provinciale dell'economia – Como, *Lineamenti e dati dell'attività economica provinciale 1927–1928–1929,* Como 1930, p. 8.

55. Barbagli, *Sotto lo stesso tetto,* p. 108–13.

56. Rossi, *Inchiesta sulla piccola proprietà,* p. 64.

57. On the so-called price 'scissors' which worked to the detriment of the agricultural sector see P. Corner, 'Fascist agrarian policy and the Italian economy in the inter-war years', in J. Davis (ed.), *Gramsci and Italy's Passive Revolution,* London 1979, p. 263.

58. Rossi, *Inchiesta sulla piccola proprietà,* passim.

59. Rossi, *Inchiesta sulla piccola proprietà,* p. 56.

60. Ibid., p. 57.

61. The 1931 population census tends to exaggerate the number of small proprietors through most of northern and central Italy. This appears to have been the result of the manipulation of census criteria in such a way as to include even those with a garden in the category of small proprietors. This was done in an attempt to claim success for fascist policies which aimed at reducing the number of politically dangerous landless labourers and stabilising them on the land as leaseholders or small proprietors (the policy of so-called *sbracciantizzazione*); see A. Marabini, 'Spostamenti di classe nelle campagne italiane', in *Lo Stato Operaio,* 1934, 7.

62. Ufficio provinciale dell'economia – Como, *Alcuni dati statistici,* p. 17.

63. Ibid., p. 16.

64. G. Rusconi, *Salviamo una industria gloriosa! I setaioli e la nazione,* Milan 1923.

65. Ufficio provinciale dell'economia – Como, *Alcuni dati statistici,* p. 24.

66. In 1928, for example, the yield fell to an average of 43 kilos of raw silk per ounce of worm eggs: ibid., p .25. Even before the war Serpieri had warned that profitable production could only be achieved with a minimum of 50 kilos per ounce and that proprietors would be wise to look for a yield of 60: MAIC, *Atti della Commissione d'inchiesta per la industria bacologica e serica,* pp. 654–5.

67. Ufficio provinciale dell'economia – Como, *Alcuni dati statistici,* p. 44.

68. Ibid.

69. Ibid: 'Only a very few firms – the strongest – have improved their factories. The great majority of businesses survive among difficulties and uncertainty ...'.

70. Prices for raw silk fell disastrously after 1926. Fresh cocoons, which had sold for L 29 kg. in 1926, went for L 2 kg. in 1934. Prices, which reflected revaluation but essentially a fall in demand on international markets, never recovered before the Second World War. See Istituto Centrale di Statistica, *Sommario di statistiche storiche italiane 1861–1955*, Rome 1958, p. 181.

71. A very rough comparison can be made with the figure for 1911 – 4,556 firms in the *circondari* of Como and Lecco; all figures are from the Industrial censuses 1911, 1927, and 1937–40.

72. If textile firms and their employees are excluded from the calculations, the remaining firms show an average size of around 9 employees in 1911, 4.2 employees in 1927, and 4.6 in 1939: ibid.

73. Ufficio provinciale dell'economia – Como, *Lineamenti e dati*, p. 8.

74. In 1927, the iron and steel, metal, and mechanical industries in the province of Como were split into 1,450 units with around 15,000 employees, the furniture industry into 2,700 units with 9,000 employees, clothing into 3,200 units with 7,600 employees, and foodstuffs into 1,100 units with 3,100 employees: ibid., p. 35.

75. P. Corner, 'Italy', in S. Salter and J. Stevenson (eds). *The Working Class and Politics in Europe and America 1929–45*, London 1989, p. 162.

76. Rossi, *Inchiesta sulla piccola proprietà*, pp.63–4: 'loans from sons, employed in industry, to their leaseholder fathers in order that they could buy land, were extremely common'.

77. On what seems to be a very similar choice of values, but operating in the 1980s among a later generation, similarly exposed to conflicts between family and wider society, see P. Allum, and I. Diamanti, *'50/'80, vent'anni. Due generazioni di giovani a confronto*, Roma 1986, pp. 393–400.

78. See P. Sabbatucci-Severino and A. Trento, 'Alcuni cenni sul mercato del lavoro durante il fascismo', in *Quaderni storici*, 29–30, 1975.

79. G. Mori, 'Materiali, temi ed ipotesi per una storia dell'industria nella regione toscana durante il fascismo (1923–39)', in (various authors), *La Toscana nel regime fascista*, Florence 1971; quoted in G. Beccatini, 'Riflessioni sullo sviluppo socio-economico della Toscana', in *Storia d'Italia, Le regioni dall'Unita ad oggi: la Toscana* (ed. G. Mori), Turin 1986, p. 911.

80. Becattini, ibid., p. 912.

81. See A. Pescarolo and G. B. Ravenna, *Il proletariato invisibile. La*

manifattura della paglia nella Toscana mezzadrile (1820–1950), Milan 1991.

82. See Lorenzoni, *Inchiesta sulla piccola proprietà. Relazione finale:*, p. 11; quoted in D. Preti, 'L'economia toscana nel periodo fascista', in *Storia d'Italia, Le regioni dall'Unità ad oggi: la Toscana* (ed. G. Mori), Turin 1986, p. 610–11.

83. Becattini, 'Riflessioni', pp. 905–09.

84. M. Forni, *Storie familiari e storie di proprietà*, Turin 1987.

5
Peasants and Entrepreneurship: From Fascism to the Present

5.1 Social and Economic Trends

The 1940s and 1950s are a period when economic and social trends which had already been put into motion during the recession years became consolidated and political culture found a new stability, adapting to the disappearance of a rural world and indeed becoming a propulsive factor in the emergence of the new industrialisation.

The first trend is a shift in employment from agriculture to industry and to the tertiary sector. Such a shift marks the end of the peasants' dream of acquiring self-sufficiency in agriculture, but it does not mean a total abandonment of the land or a process of urbanisation. In the province of Como the transition to an industrial society benefited the countryside just as much as the main towns (Como and Lecco), and was not accompanied by any marked process of territorial and financial concentration of firms. The new industrialisation was as diffused as the old one, taking advantage of local entrepreneurship and small capital inputs.

The second trend is a substantial increase in the number of men employed as wage-earners in the manufacturing sector, while the number of female workers remains substantially static in absolute terms but diminishes in relative terms. This development could easily be interpreted as the final stage of a transition from peasants to proletarians; but instead it represented only the pre-final phase of a different type of process.

The third and dominant trend is the transition from peasants to entrepreneurs, which resumed in the 1950s and 1960s after an initial but short-lived 'wave' in the 1930s. Although we refer basically to the same phenomenon, there are important qualitative differences between the first and the second 'waves' of small entrepreneurship, separated by the return to a democratic political system and free trade. In the fascist period, and particularly in the 1930s and early 1940s, the drive towards entrepreneurship was socially-based rather than market-led; also, motivations were primarily of a negative character. In the 1950s and 1960s the drive was both socially-based and market-led: push *and* pull factors were both at work. These differences need to be looked at in some detail, as they will provide an explanation for the astounding resilience and dynamism of the small business sector, against all odds, fifty years on.

At the centre of both trends is the family, which succeeds in internalising and thus neutralising the possible disruptive effects of economic change, just as it had done in the nineteenth century at the time of the development of the silk industry. It is thanks to pluriactivity that the transition to industrial work is not experienced as a dramatic or traumatic one. Family structure, of course, is itself subject to change: the family experiences a transition from peasant–worker to worker–peasant. However, this transition, which in the previous century had been a prelude to a process of proletarianisation as well as political militancy on the part of these families and in particular of their male heads, now became the springboard for social mobility. The reason for this is to be found both in new market opportunities and in increased capital resources within each family, two factors which had been present only on a very limited scale in the nineteenth century.

In order to understand these trends we need to go back to the fascist period. As we have already seen, this was a time when local sharecroppers, in the space of twenty-odd years, first joined the ranks of the small landowners, finally crowning a century-old aspiration, and then were brought abruptly to the realisation that possession of the land did not guarantee them self-sufficiency.

5.2 The Marginalisation of Agriculture

From 1936 onwards the number of people employed in agriculture continued to drop, becoming totally negligible by 1981 (Table 5.1).

Table 5.1 Number and Percentages of People Employed in Agriculture, 1936 to 1981

Year:	1936	1951	1981
Total numbers	58,685	35,448	7,827
As a percentage of the total active population	23.9	13.6	2.4
Males	44,630	30,615	6,017
Females	14,055	4,833	1,810

Source: ISTAT Population Censuses.

The loss of importance of the agricultural sector took some time to be properly acknowledged by the local population and the relevant fascist authorities. After the First World War, in fact, the most important trend had seemed to be that of great social mobility within the primary sector, brought about by a crisis of the sharecropping system.

In the aftermath of the war, as we saw in the previous chapter, social mobility derived mainly from the pressure brought on employers by organised peasant struggles backed by socialist and Catholic leagues. Later, it was due to economic recession, in particular to the fall in cocoon prices and the loss of markets for local silk-production. As a result people gave up agricultural work as their main occupation in increasing numbers, while employers had to offer more favourable contracts to retain their workforce, or sold off part of their estates. By 1936 it was clear that only the newly formed category of small landowners persisted in believing that they could make a living for themselves and their families out of the land. This explains why, in a province where land fragmentation was already in process and pluriactivity well established, the number of heads of families who considered themselves first and foremost landowning farmers grew in the middle of the recession both in absolute and in real terms, as Table 5.2 shows:

Table 5.2 Independent and Dependent Households in the Primary Sector

Year	1921	1936	1951
Independent rural households (head is landowner/tenant farmer)	25,508	32,649	24,299
Dependent rural households (sharecroppers/labourers)	41,771	4,676	2,652
Independent rural households as a percentage of total households	18.7	22.5	12.9

Source: ISTAT Population Censuses.

Table 5.2 also shows that in 1951 the number of heads of families registered as landowners had considerably fallen. This does not mean that the process of land fragmentation had been successfully reversed. The *Inchiesta Medici* of 1951 records a very high number of privately owned plots for the province of Como, and an even higher number of landowners. Altogether, there were 138,465 landholdings in the province at that date, and an average of two landowners per holding; 89.7 per cent of all landholdings covered less than two hectares and 7.5 per cent less than five.[1] If we recall that there were 150,000 families in the province at the same date, we can have an idea of how widespread landownership had become. Nor was the phenomenon restricted to the mountain areas, where traditionally landholding was very fragmented. As the Inchiesta puts it:

> In the hills and highlands [of Lombardy] a marked tendency towards land fragmentation got under way at the start of the century and accelerated after the First World War. The aristocracy, which owned the land up to the very end of the last century, was partly responsible for this process, being unable to carry out the new functions required by landholding. However, the rapidity with which it all happened was due above all to the formation in these areas of numerous industries, which allowed local sharecropping families – increasingly becoming mixed urban – rural communities – to save money. This in turn allowed them to buy the long-since-desired piece of land and to solve their basic consumption problems, particularly at times of crisis. Thus in these areas countless small landholdings were created, often no larger than vegetable plots and only rarely forming self-sufficient farming units.[2]

The crucial issue, however, is precisely that each family did not own enough land to make a living out of it, and that from the 1930s onwards the reality of this situation was acknowledged by the families themselves. This is why in the 1951 census the majority of households gave a non-agricultural activity as their main occupation. The transition from peasant-worker to worker-peasant families was now complete throughout the province.

It is interesting to note that the path followed by the Como and Lecco farmers was the same which had been followed by the Varese ones five decades earlier. In other words the peasant in the peasant–worker/worker–peasant transition is not a sharecropper but a landholder or, conversely, a landless labourer. This confirms once again that the sharecropper represents a socially static figure (though one capable of capital accumulation), who becomes an agent of social change only when he becomes proletarianised or, paradoxically, when he fulfils his hopes of rising to the status of landowner. It is then that, given the inadequate size of his holding, he is faced with precarious survival and takes on a second activity, usually with a view to sustain what he still consider his main one, i.e. farming. When the income from his 'subsidiary' activity overcomes that from farming his perceptions change and he is ready to consider work on the land as a subsidiary activity only.

For the above reasons the increase in the number of independent farmers in the 1920s and 1930s must be considered as the sign of a society in transition rather than that of a new social order. The new order, if anything, is that which emerges from the 1951 census, which shows a prevalence of industrial wage-earning families. This is connected with the second trend we referred to, viz. the growing employment of men as wage-earners in the manufacturing sector. Yet even this trend is not a true picture of the new society. In the fascist period, as we shall now see, wage-labour failed to expand to the extent that most households became dependent on it and gave up alternative sources of income. On the contrary, households were forced to take up marginal fallback occupations on a self-employed basis. Later, there were new opportunities for employment as wage-earners, in the areas above Milan if not at home, but the survival of households as individual enterprises during fascism prevented wage-labour from becoming the dominant mode of production. Most families, as we saw, owned a plot of land, and often their old farmhouse as well. They were not independent farmers, but neither were they proletarian workers earning a family wage. More importantly, they showed a propensity to go into self-employment. Social mobility resumed in the post-war period, this time proving long-lived.

5.3 The Fascist Precedent

The third economic and social trend of the post-war period, i.e. the transition from peasant to entrepreneur, also has a precedent in the fascist period, though even in this case the 1930s created more the illusion of change than the making of a new social order. In particular, although small entrepreneurial activity can be clearly detected in the 1920s and 1930s, it represented mainly a socially-driven rather than market-led phenomenon, which was due to economic recession, industrial and agricultural unemployment and the increasing need on the part of the newly-formed 'independent' farmers to prop up their failing incomes. In contrast, the entrepreneurship of the 1950s and 1960s was both socially-driven and market-led – pull as well as push factors were at work, the return to free trade and the opening up of export markets creating a dynamic economy which was markedly different from the autarkic one of the fascist period.

It is well known that at times of recession the rate of firm-formation goes up. This is true now as it was in the 1930s. However, the sustainability of this kind of entrepreneurial activity must be seriously put in doubt. Higher rates of small-firm formation may simply reflect the recession itself: small firms emerge to some extent as the result of desperation on the part of those made redundant or expelled from agriculture, and may be set up most frequently in industries in economic decline, since these have low start-up costs. The self-exploitation of the family and low wages are often all that is required.

This seems to sum up precisely what happened in the late 1920s and 1930s. As traditional sources of income – from cocoons and raw silk production to female and child labour in the silk-mills – dried up, peasant-worker families in the Lecco and Como area started to look for alternative forms of employment, just as at Varese and Cantù in the previous century. Work in industrial plants as wage-earners was an immediate prospect, and it was taken up, albeit reluctantly. Industry, however, was stagnating, and it could not absorb all those expelled from agriculture. Men had better chances of finding work in industry than women in those days; but their growing employment as wage-earners was accompanied by a process of expulsion of women workers from the declining textiles sector. Overall, people with industrial occupations rose only marginally between 1921 and 1936, from 129,383 to 138,101.[3] Male workers increased from roughly 60,000 to 80,000, while women workers decreased from about 65,000 to 55,000.

Even those who could find work in industry were in a very precarious position. Fascism had a policy of preventing rural workers from emigrating to the towns in search of work, and fascist unions felt their duty was to defend and protect the employment of existing urban workers, who were potentially more dangerous because more politicised and with a tradition of militancy. Both the unions and the fascist party staged a campaign putting pressure on employers to make workers from the countryside redundant in precedence over long-standing, urban-based employees. This applied particularly to commuting workers who did not reside in the place where they worked.[4] In addition, seasonal emigration abroad, to France and Switzerland, had become more difficult, in part because of fascist policies directed at discouraging this practice, but mainly because of falling demand for migrant labour.

In short, push factors mobilised peasant–worker and worker–peasant families alike, the former because of low cocoon prices and unemployment in the silk industry, as well as having to repay loans and debts incurred in acquiring their plot of land, the latter because of the loss of the traditional safety-valve of temporary emigration, and the increasing lay-offs in the large industrial plants north of Milan. They reacted to this situation by taking on extra work on a self-employed basis: both men and women were 'activated' to earn that vital extra income. A very large number of the small firms listed in the 1936 census are no more than one-man, or one-woman, operations. Many more have only one employee (presumably very often the husband or wife, or another member of the family). The activities themselves reflect in part continuing links with an agricultural background and in part more recent contacts with commerce and manufacturing. Thus women washed laundry, ironed, sewed, made laces, opened a café or a food shop; men made or mended shoes, worked with wood and prepared sausages and salami for sale rather than for their own consumption. Others became makers of clothing (tailors and seamstresses), produced paper, called themselves hairdressers or barbers, and generally added to the myriad of small activities which characterised the moment. The number of women involved in these activities is notable. Occupations of this kind had less to do with market needs than with existing skills on offer and the availability of local resources. A working farm could easily form the basis for trading farm produce, either to retailers or by selling it in the towns; a farmhouse could become a rudimentary food-processing plant. The Vismara firm, for example, today a major industrial complex, developed in the 1930s as a producer of cold pork meat (sausages and salami).[5]

It is not surprising, therefore, that many new small enterprises were formed in traditional artisanal sectors – chasing an unchanged and possibly even shrinking number of customers – or in agriculturally-related activities. Out of 16,888 registered self-employed in the industrial sector in 1936, a quarter were in woodworking, slightly less than a quarter in food-processing, and a third in clothing.[6] Apart from woodworking, which had originated at the start of the century in the area around Cantù in response to both market needs and unstable rural conditions, and had become increasingly industrially oriented, the other two activities were predominantly made up of artisanal occupations. 'Clothing' included tailors, laundry-washers, barbers and hairdressers, while food-processing listed bakers, millers and cake-makers, i.e. occupations which now would be considered as part of the service, not the manufacturing sector.

The general confusion between manufacturing, commercial, and service activities is perhaps typical of a population in transition and uncertain of its own identity, particularly in respect of a census form. Generally, commerce saw a growth in catering and the retailing of foods, and the running of hotels and cafés. Out of 9,663 registered self-employed in the service sector proper, more than a third were food caterers and more than a quarter were food retailers.[7] A large number of people were registered simply as travelling salesmen – people who may have been simply street pedlars, but were more likely perhaps to represent the first examples of the rickety-van market trader, who moved on a daily basis from local market to local market, to end up (sometimes rich, usually just getting by) immortalised in the post-war films of neo-realism. Clearly commerce in the region was growing, despite general difficulties (the region was passing, after all, from an essentially pre-commercial era to one in which small-scale commerce became generalised) and offered opportunities for those with initiative and imagination.

The industrial census of 1937–40 confirms that the vast majority of small enterprises were in the above sectors. Altogether, they made up 63 per cent of the total number of industrial plants (10,204 out of 16,203). The vast majority consisted of the owner-manager himself (or herself) and no more than one employee, as Table 5.3 shows.

Table 5.3 Firms and Workers by Size of Firm in the Food, Clothing, Leather and Wood Industries (1937–40)

Size of firm (no. employed):	0–1		2–5		6–10		11–100		101+	
	No. of Firms	No. of Workers	No. of Firms	No. of Workers	No. of Firms	No. of Workers	No. of Firms	No of Workers	No. of Firms	No of Workers
Food Ind	1,336	815	1,039	2,602	64	457	29	506	2	638
Leather	925	925	243	618	16	116	11	358	2	664
Clothing	2,193	2,192	458	1,166	40	273	27	833	2	857
Woodwork	1,557	1,549	1,177	3,393	149	1,063	78	1,741	4	912

Source: ISTAT Industrial Census.

Excepting woodworking, a long-standing industry with a well-established market reaching out to the regional capital, Milan, less than half of these newly created small businesses survived beyond the fascist period (Table 5.4).

Table 5.4 Firms and Workers in the Food, Leather, and Clothing Industries (1937–40 and 1951)

	1937–40		1951	
	Firms	Workers	Firms	Workers
Food Industry	3,285	5,148	522	3,944
Leather	1,197	2,726	50	229
Clothing	2,720	5,220	2,482	5,892
Total	7,202	13, 094	3,054	10,006

Source: ISTAT Industrial Censuses.

The above tables indicate quite clearly the micro and marginal nature of the entrepreneurial activity of the 1930s. It was by and large entrepreneurship by default, the result of the break-up of the agricultural-silk cycle in the absence of viable alternatives for integration of family incomes. It did not come about in response to changes in demand or even to an increased demand for traditional consumer goods/services, but simply to bad economic times. In some respects this type of small-firm formation was only another expression of pluriactivity, in the sense that it aimed at raising a bit of extra income for the family, with little or no capital investment apart from family labour. Whatever surplus the family had accumulated, in fact, had in most cases already been spent on land purchase. Since full-time farming was proving untenable, the capital spent on acquiring a plot of land was not bearing any fruits. This, among other factors, explains the family's determination to put the land to some other use than farming and to make money on the side.

On the positive side, the micro-entrepreneurship of this period reflects the determination on the part of local families to sort themselves out of the recession, making use of relief or help from the State and charity organisations whenever offered, but generally relying on their networks of families and friends. The burden of unemployment was borne entirely by local families, the loss of wages on the part of one or more of their members being compensated for by the redoubled efforts of those who were lucky enough to keep their jobs or, as we have just seen, contrived to market their 'domestic' skills. As a fascist report on the provincial economic situation in August 1932 put it: 'The mass of unemployed local people does not seriously affect public order, both because of timely public relief measures, particularly those directed to the most needy, and because in the majority of cases not all members of the same family are unemployed, so that in each household there continues to be sufficient income for subsistence needs.'[8]

Thus the 1930s marked to some extent a direct transition from farmers to (precarious) entrepreneurs in largely non-industrial or only marginally industrial sectors. It could not have been otherwise, for these were people without the necessary expertise or contacts to set up a small firm of their own in industries of which they had little or no knowledge. They turned to self-employment in occupations which provided a continuity with activities they were used to.

A more direct link between the entrepreneurship of the 1930s and that of the 1950s and 1960s can be found in the expansion of the two sectors which were to sustain the development of the post-war period, i.e. the building and mechanical industries. Between 1927 and 1937–40 these sectors expanded considerably in terms of employees, and the number of new enterprises by and large kept up with the expansion of the workforce, although there was a modest but significant shift towards plant concentration (Table 5. 5).

Table 5.5 The Expansion of the Mechanical and Building Industries, 1927-1937

	1927		1937–40	
	Firms	Workers	Firms	Workers
Mechanical Industry	1,194	9,163	1,585	18,933
Building Industry	576	6,373	922	12,577

Source: ISTAT Industrial Censuses.

Even in these 'modern' sectors, however, new firm-formation seems to have suffered the same precariousness and fragility which affected entrepreneurial activity in the more traditional artisanal occupations. Many new firms in the metal and mechanical sector, for example, typically produced low-quality articles, such as rivets, washers, nails, screws, nuts and bolts, metal hinges, steel wires and rods, bicycle spokes, struts for umbrellas, etc., which required little capital investment and which often relied on the reworking of scrap. Most of these new firms were very small and were probably little more than backyard industries employing only one or two people. Indeed, the majority of firms were micro rather than small, and survived at the margins of the large firms. In the 1930s, in fact, a marked dualism existed within these industries between a large number of very small firms (with fewer than ten employees) accounting for only a small percentage of total employees at one end, and a handful of large firms accounting for a large share of the total workforce on the other. Table 5.6 illustrates this dualism:

Table 5.6 Firms and Workers by Size of Firm in the Mechanical and Building Industries in 1937–40 (Percentages)

Size of firm by workers	0–10		11–100		251+	
	Firms	Workers	Firms	Workers	Firms	Workers
Mechanical Industry	80%	15%	80%	38%	0.5%	35%
Building Industry	86%	17%	10%	25%	1%	40%

Source: ISTAT Industrial Census.

When considered against the background of the 1930s, the post-war development, as we shall now see, gave the local people the chance of establishing their entrepreneurial activity on a surer footing and put the small firm squarely at the centre of the local economy.

5.4 Post-War Economic Development

The new entrepreneurial drive of the post-war period was to come from the second generation, i.e. from the sons of the ex-farmers who increasingly went to work as wage-earners in a factory or a building site as the economy started to revive. They were able to acquire the necessary expertise to contemplate setting up on their own in the same industry where they worked. The transition from peasant to entrepreneur, which had taken place directly in the fascist period and had proved short-lived, was now tried indirectly, with people becoming industrial workers before attempting to go into self-employment. Whereas new firm-formation in the first case took place largely in areas outside industrial manufacturing, as we saw, in the second instance it stemmed from manufacturing itself, and it has since contributed to its continuing growth by providing key strategic functions such as marketing, design, technical and managerial consultancy and accountancy services.

In short, the direct transition peasant-to-entrepreneur represented an extension of the old economic and social order, leading to an expansion of agriculturally-related and traditional artisanal occupations as well as services to consumers. The indirect transition peasant-to-industrial worker-to-entrepreneur created a new industrial order, of which use of the land, manufacturing activities and services are all components.

Let us look more closely at the economic development of the post-war period.

The marginalisation of agriculture continued at a fast pace, while the industrial sector expanded considerably in absolute terms but decreased in relative terms, and the tertiary sector 'took off', as can be seen from Table 5.7.

Table 5.7 Active Population by Sectors, 1936 to 1981 (Percentages)

Agriculture			Industry			Services		
1936	1951	1981	1936	1951	1981	1936	1951	1981
23%	14%	2%	58%	63%	57%	19%	23%	41%

Source: ISTAT Population Census.

The resilience of the industrial sector is truly remarkable, considering that the province has had to face up to a continuing loss of employment in its oldest sector, that of textiles, and that new technologies have increasingly made it possible to replace labour with machinery. The expansion has been due primarily to the mechanical and building industries (Table 5.8).

Table 5.8 Relative Weight of the Textiles, Mechanical, Building and Wood Industries within the Manufacturing Sector, 1951–1981 (Percentages)

	1951		1981	
	Firms	Workers	Firms	Workers
Total Numbers	10,451	114,741	22,458	176,913
Textiles	14%	42%	6%	18%
Mechanical Industry	20%	20%	24%	33%
Building	9%	7%	28%	12%
Woodworking	29%	8%	16%	10%

Source: ISTAT Industrial Censuses.

In stark contrast to the 1930s, in the mechanical, building and textiles industries small firms are now the norm: firms with up to 100 employees in 1981 accounted for the largest share of both plants and employees, while large firms (with more than 500 employees) had become negligible (Table 5.9).

Table 5.9 Firms and Workers by Size of Firm in the Mechanical, Building and Textiles Industries, 1936–1981 (Percentages)

	1936				1981			
Size by workers	0-100		500+		0-100		500+	
	F	W	F	W	F	W	F	W
Building	98%	53%	0.2%	27%	99%	95%	0%	0%
Mechanical	96%	42%	0.3%	23%	98%	63%	1.5%	12.0%
Textiles	98%	32%	0.1%	16%	94%	63%	0.1%	1.7%

Source: ISTAT Industrial Censuses.

Consequently, the number of firms in these sectors has grown considerably: the drive towards entrepreneurship and self-employment was therefore as high after the war as it had been in the 1930s, with the important difference that market needs directly stimulated economic expansion.

In the post-war period wood and metal industrial components were in heavy demand, thanks to the reconstruction and the need for new houses. Local demands for bicycles and motorbikes, as well as spare parts and repairs was also high, given the increasing army of commuters who travelled to work every day. At Lecco, and in the nearby villages, metal production had always been an important source of income; in a myriad of small workshops and factories people traditionally made scissors, nails, hammers and agricultural and domestic tools. Now they and others could produce chains, wheels and other spare parts for popular means of transport, as well as handles, hinges, locks, blinds and other components for the building industry.

Entrepreneurship by choice, fuelled by economic expansion, replaced entrepreneurship by default, embarked on at times of recession. Sheer hard work, family support and the exploitation of a piece of land for both consumption and living and work premises as well as security against bank loans continued to form crucial supply-side factors in promoting entrepreneurship. The trend towards economic expansion based on the creation of new small businesses is well documented by local sources, which in some cases also give interesting accounts of how it was achieved. One such account can be found in a Report by a Parliamentary Commission of Enquiry on Unemployment, published in 1953. According to the report there were 11,000 unemployed textile workers in the province of Como, owing to a stagnant demand for textile and particularly silk products. However, the report added that the difficulties incurred by Como textile firms were also to be attributed to

> the installation of roughly 10,000 looms in the homes of families previously employed by local silk factories. These looms are in operation for longer hours than those fixed by law. It is a kind of activity which manages to avoid tax and social security payments. The present state of affairs was caused by the industrialists, who when proceeding to renovate their machinery made the serious mistake of selling off their old looms to local artisans. These in turn, thanks to a few minor repairs, put the looms back into full working order and became large industry's direct competitors.[9]

Thus domestic looms reappeared in individual homes or in garden sheds and remained active day and night, thanks to the self-exploitation of the entire family. These 'self-employed' provided the infantry which allowed silk weaving to fight back and survive. Their aspiration to achieve economic independence and to move socially upwards meant that this sector had found a new supply of abundant and relatively cheap labour. The employers' own motives, in fact, may have been quite different from those indicated in the report. Selling off their looms to existing employees may have been a very economic way to ensure cheaper and trouble-free forms of labour. There was probably a mutual advantage in this move towards industrial de-structuring, though it may well be true that some of the new artisans/entrepreneurs were proving more successful than anticipated and capable of competing with their old employers. Incidentally, this intense local competition also helped the silk industry to revive, moving towards the manufacturing of high-quality cloths destined for a luxury market, mainly in the United States. Indeed, after 1960 Como had the satisfaction of beating its long-standing rival and competitor, Lyons, and of remaining the only major silk centre in the whole of Europe.

Another, more personal account of the new entrepreneurship has been given by a local self-employed artisan, interviewed in the early 1980s as part of a research project for the University of Milan:

At the same time those workers who were professionally trained, the most able, the most adventurous, the most forward-looking among them, started to become self-employed. They were growing like mushrooms, and they were artisans and at the same time farmers. These were people who started at 4 in the morning, or at 5 if they were lucky, they worked on the land and then they would become artisans, working all day, mainly as furniture makers ... And in the evening they resumed their work on the land, looking after their cattle, or gathering the hay ... perhaps till 9-10 at night. Thus these people worked 15–16 hours per day. They did this until they became certain that their other activity, as artisans, small entrepreneurs, had reached a certain stability; after that, gradually, there came the abandonment of farming. Some time after the development of furniture making, the metal industry also began to develop or, as in my case, the making of metal parts for the furniture industry ...[10]

It is interesting to note that the above informant mentioned professional training as one of the characteristics of the new entrepreneurs. The supply-side factors recalled earlier, however important, were clearly no longer sufficient preconditions for going into self-employment, at least in those sectors which required more sophisticated tools and machinery than just a weaving loom. To them one should add industrial experience, useful work contacts and above all human inventiveness. Indeed Brusco, when explaining the success of small firms in present-day Italian industrial districts, made explicit reference to the capacity to innovate and the inventiveness shown by workers and artisans/entrepreneurs alike.[11] The Brianza informant confirmed this characteristic with reference to his area: 'These artisans are people who struggled a lot, each one of them has his own story, a story of sacrifice, of really hard work, of risks ... They are people who, some more than others, were inventors, each of them in his own way created something, had their moment of glory.'[12]

Recent research carried out by one of the authors on small textile firms in the Como area has also shown that many of the entrepreneurs of the 1950s and 1960s were self-made men, with few formal qualifications but a good running knowledge of their industry and of the technical – as opposed to the marketing/ commercial – aspects of manufacturing. Most of them still take pride in being actively and personally involved in the production process, refusing to take on a more managerial and directorial role.[13]

Between 1971 and 1981 firm size continued to decrease, largely following a nation-wide pattern, because of a need for higher flexibility and the application of new technologies to ever-smaller units of production. In the same decade the tertiary sector took on a new supportive role for local manufacturing, managing the interface between local producers and outside buyers, as well as providing the necessary financial backing. The changed composition of the services industry can be seen from Table 5.10.

Table 5.10 The Commercial and Financial Sector in the Post-War Period

	1951		1971		1981	
	Firms	Workers	Firms	Workers	Firms	Workers
Wholesaling	1,076	3,460	1,466	7,161	2,225	10,475
Retailing	6,769	13,266	10,836	20,713	11,295	23,579
Catering	2,944	6,181	3,405	7,426	3,332	9,247
Commerce Intermediaries	405	531	233	465	2,067	2,508
Credit	114	892	179	2,010	255	3,932
Services to Firms	120	216	81	206	3,347	7,785
Goods/Vehicles Repairs	—	—	—	—	2,132	5,178
Total	11,514	25,199	16,448	38,687	24,750	62,925

Source: ISTAT Industrial Censuses.

The relative weight of wholesaling and retailing decreased from 68 per cent in 1951 to 54.6 per cent in 1981, and that of the catering industry from 25.6 per cent to 13.4 per cent, while the relative weight of commerce intermediaries went up in the same period from 0.2 per cent to 4 per cent and that of financial services from 3.5 per cent to 6.3 per cent. If we take into account the fact that the two categories 'Goods and vehicles repairs' and 'Services to firms' appeared for the first time as separate categories in the tertiary sector in the 1981 census, while in previous censuses they probably counted as part of the manufacturing sector, we can conclude that roughly half of all plants and employees registered in the 1981 Industrial Census as part of the tertiary sector were in fact closely linked to and providing invaluable support for local manufacturing. In many cases they represent functions which vertically integrated manufacturing firms normally carry in-house, but which Como manufacturers prefer to 'buy in' from small independent local firms. This in itself represents an important step forward, because local small firms, as we said earlier, used to be very product-oriented, believing, often with good reason, that their products would easily sell, thanks to their fine quality and competitive prices. This meant neglecting those functions, such as research and development and marketing, which increasingly have come to determine whether a particular product is chosen and bought in preference to others. Incidentally, the category 'services to firms' employed in 1981 about 10 per cent of the total services workforce, a figure on a par with that recorded for the province of Milan, which includes, of course, such a highly developed commercial and tertiary centre as the city of Milan itself.

Indeed, the most significant difference from the entrepreneurship of the 1930s is probably the increasing interpenetration, in the post-war period, of the 'manufacturing' with the 'commercial' sector, so much so that to consider them separately is now almost meaningless. In the 1930s these two sectors seemed to lead separate existences; the commercial sector was made up predominantly of food retailers and restaurateurs. In the post-war period there was a great expansion of self-employed sales agents and market intermediaries and, more recently, of providers of specialist services.

The age-composition of the self-employed by sector throws into clearer relief how entrepreneurship took place in generational 'waves'. Census data show that only 38 per cent of self-employed artisans and entrepreneurs in the more traditional sectors (textiles, food-processing, furniture-making etc.), were aged less than forty in 1981. In mechanical industry the percentage of younger entrepreneurs was 47 per cent and in the 'services to firms' sector a high 56 per cent. These young entrepreneurs are generally much better qualified than the older ones, and have set up their enterprise as a 'spin-off' from an existing firm. Many others, particularly in the more traditional sectors, have inherited their firm; compared to their fathers, they seem to possess a much more 'comprehensive' awareness of what a firm is and of the importance of strategic functions such as design, marketing and distribution.

As new generations of entrepreneurs replace the old ones, one can detect a significant shift towards specialist activities in the services sector, while the more traditional manufacturing sectors appear to be 'ageing'. Yet, as we mentioned earlier, to divide the local economy into separate sectors is largely misleading.

For the above reasons the local economy today appears like a complex but coherent structure whose different parts are meaningful only when they are considered in relation to each other. It is this internal cohesiveness that has enabled local small businesses to become competitive in world markets and to perpetuate their 'smallness' as an independent form of industrial organisation. The dualism between micro and large firms which was apparent in the fascist period has been eliminated; there is now a continuum from very small to small to medium firms, with the large firms representing almost a rare feature. The full implications of the existence of a 'grey area' between economic sectors and the unique organisational traits of this kind of small-scale industry will be discussed in the next chapter.

5.5 Como Today: Entrepreneurship and Society

The economic and social trends described in the previous section have now come to the end of their cycle. The agricultural sector, as we have just seen, plays only a very minor role in the economy of northern Lombardy and employs a negligible percentage of the active population. It no longer constitutes a propulsive factor for entrepreneurial activity: there are no more peasants who aspire to upward social mobility. Entrepreneurship, however, remains the most characteristic trait of the local people, and it appears to be still rooted in the pluriactive family and the community to which the family feels it belongs. To illustrate this, we need to look at the ways in which the relationship between economy and society has evolved since the post-war period.

It seems appropriate to start by giving some indications as to the size and characteristics of Como's entrepreneurship today in comparison to that of forty years ago. On the basis of the population censuses, and excluding the agricultural sector, the number of self-employed artisans and entrepreneurs rose from 33,262 in 1951 to 59,469 in 1981 – in percentage terms, from 12.6 to 16.6 per cent of the total active population in industry and commerce. On the basis of the industrial censuses the figure was 37,223 (or 23.6 per cent of the active population excluding agriculture) in 1951 and rose to 76,209 in 1981 (26 per cent). The difference between the two censuses reflects the 'pluriactive' nature of many families: the population census, in fact, is compiled according to each family's own statement, while the industrial census registers all business partners and – as a separate category – all family helpers. As many business 'partners' (often family members) and family helpers may also have other jobs – either as moonlighters or to sustain the business

From Peasant to Entrepreneur

in its initial stage – they do not list themselves as 'self-employed' in the population census.

A better indicator to quantify self-employment in the province is provided by the number of households registered as such in the population census, as the data refer to the head of family rather than to all its members. The head of family is, in fact, much more likely to run the business as a full-time job, while the various adult members of his family engage in other activities and only work in the business on a part-time or seasonal basis. Table 5.11 provides the relevant data.

Table 5.11 Self-Employed and Wage-Earning Households in 1951 and 1981

	1951	1981
Self-employed households		
(excluding agriculture)	20,994	37,269
as per cent of total households	18.6	26.0
Wage-earning households		
(excluding agriculture) as	60,623	71,224
per cent of total households	53.8	48.9
Self-employed households		
as per cent of wage-earning		
households	34.6	52.3

Source: ISTAT Population Censuses.

Table 5.11 shows that between 1951 and 1981 self-employed households almost doubled, while wage-earning ones increased by only a sixth, and in fact declined in relative terms. As a result in 1981 there was one self-employed household for every two wage-earning ones, whereas in 1951 there had been one in every three.

It should be added here that in 1981 the percentage of self-employed people (or households) out of the total active population does not accurately reflect the increased weight gained by this social group in their local community. The reason for this is that in the 1970s there was considerable *immigration* to this province from other parts of Italy. In 1981 a fifth of the resident population aged 19–64 were from other regions of Italy, the vast majority from the South. Most immigrants found employment as industrial wage-earners or State employees; very few of them became entrepreneurs or self-employed. This is indirectly confirmed by A. Bull's recent survey of small textile firms at and around Como.[14] Out of fifty owners/managers contacted in the area, only two had been born outside the Lombard region, one in Istanbul, the other in Brazil (probably with locally-born parents emigrated to those countries). Some 41 per cent had been born in the same village where their firm was; 28 per cent in another village within the province's boundaries and 26 per cent in a nearby locality, situated in a neighbouring province. In short, entrepreneurship remains an 'indigenous' phenomenon, born out of local social relations and cultural values. It may be postulated that the two phenomena are connected: the move of the local people towards self-employment, coupled with economic expansion, created the need to fill workplaces with an 'outside' labour force.

As well as locally born, entrepreneurship remains geographically diffused, so that the majority of the population are able to continue to live and work in their native villages and towns. Census data show that in 1981 still only 23 per cent of the total provincial population lived in towns with more than 20,000 inhabitants (Como, Lecco, Cantù). In addition, there was a remarkably close relationship between the distribution of the population across the province and the share of economically active people and economic firms each town is able to command, as Table 5.12 shows.

Table 5.12 Percentages of the Total Population, Economically Active People, and Firms in the Largest Towns of the Province

Towns	% of provincial population	% of active population	% of firms
Como	12.6	12.0	14.1
Lecco	6.7	6.2	6.8
Cantù	4.7	4.9	5.9
Erba	2.1	2.0	2.2
Mariano C.	2.4	2.4	2.9
Merate	1.8	1.7	1.5

Source: ISTAT Population Census

In view of the very even distribution of people and economic activities it was not surprising to find out that in 1981 in this province 86 per cent of all working people took on average no more than thirty minutes to get to their place of work – and a staggering 65 per cent employed no longer than fifteen minutes. People working in industry fared if anything better than the other categories: 88 per cent employed no more than thirty minutes (and 67 per cent no more than fifteen) to reach their workplace.

The persistence of pluriactive families is much more difficult to prove. Census data are not very helpful in this respect. They tend to show that nuclear, as opposed to extended families, are now the norm; but this piece of information is only to be expected, since families today have the means to buy or rent their own house and prefer to live separately. It would be wrong, however, to assume that inter- and intra-generational family ties have been weakened. Families may live separately but also in very close proximity. Above all, their contribution to the success of the family firm does not depend on sharing the same household, but on pooling incomes and resources.

Despite its shortcomings, the 1981 census does in fact provide some indication that families, even though predominantly nuclear, continue to rely on more than one income and on inter-generational ties. Census data show that a third of all 'children' still living at home were aged eighteen and over and that they were mostly unmarried. The total figure (96,629) roughly equalled the total number of unmarried people in the province aged 18–49 (109,364). Thus almost all unmarried people over eighteen (the vast majority aged 18–30) as well as virtually all children below that age lived at home. At that date over 80 per cent of people aged 20–29 and roughly 50 per cent of people aged 14–19 were in employment.

As was to be expected, the vast majority of people below thirty (87 per cent) were employed as wage-earners or white-collar workers, while the older generation was much more likely to have gone into self-employment (44 per cent of people aged forty and over were entrepreneurs or self-employed). Conversely, we estimated that little less than a third of all wage-earners were people aged less than twenty-five. As they got older they would have had a good chance to raise their social status by setting up a business of their own.

The above data, though unsatisfactory, seem to provide some confirmation that (a) children stay at home until they marry, almost irrespective of their age; (b) from the age of fourteen onwards most of them are not a burden to their families but provide them with extra revenues; and (c) young people tend to have relatively low-status occupations, yet they often belong to families whose status is higher than their own and have a good chance to improve their status later on in their lives.

Information gained from the above-mentioned survey of Como's small textile industrialists shows very clearly the complex interweaving between the family, the community and economic activity, as well as providing some, though far from conclusive, support for the role the whole family plays when the head decides to go into self-employment. Nearly half of owners/managers contacted claimed that relatives provided them with practical help in building up the business and almost a third said that other relatives of theirs also run their own firms. The vast majority of firms were family-owned.

When we asked owners-managers whether they gave at least some consideration to extra-professional criteria when employing new people, 36 per cent replied that they accorded some degree of preference to their own relatives, 39 per cent to relatives of their colleagues and 58 per cent to relatives of existing employees.[15] Also, with reference to choosing a new supplier or subcontractor, 76 per cent claimed that they accorded at least some preference to local business people known to them (45 per cent actually stated that they much preferred to rely on a local business person as supplier/subcontractor).

It was also discovered that the vast majority of the Como entrepreneurs contacted (74 per cent) had no wish to move their firm to another locality, while 58 per cent did not want to make it any larger. Small size, family connections and attachment to a particular locality (community) thus seem as important today as in the post-war period.

To sum up, the creation of a myriad of small, family-owned firms in the post-war period was the outcome of a particular, historically determined social form; but it also created, in the process, a specific economic form (diffused industrialisation). Both forms have been able to adjust to and internalise change without endangering their own existence. On the contrary, they successfully gave rise to a political culture which was itself a historical creation but also represented an original synthesis of the local model of development. It is to political culture that we will now turn our attention.

5.6 Diffused Industry and Political Culture

The roots of northern Lombardy's political culture, which consisted, in the second post-war period, of a 'renovated' political Catholicism and in recent days has inspired the phenomenon of 'Leghismo' (see below), can be found in the period between the two World Wars, in the same period, that is, when diffused entrepreneurship originated.

Compared to the period before the First World War, the crucial difference in families' outlook was their attitude to change. In the nineteenth and early twentieth centuries, as we saw in previous chapters, family-related mobilisation was generally of a defensive nature, i.e. to defend the semi-independent status of peasant families against the threat of proletarianisation. Not surprisingly, change was equated with the process of proletarianisation itself and therefore resisted. This is where the Catholic subculture provided a valuable source of support. After the First World War there was a transition from a primarily defensive mobilisation to one directed at altering the existing social order. Far from resisting change, rural industrial families now mobilised to speed it up and they began to appreciate the relationship between cultural formation and social change.

This is not to say that the new attitude adopted by rural/industrial families towards political culture represents a complete break with the past. One of the striking features of political culture in northern Lombardy is the ability of peasant–worker/worker–peasant families to relate to different cultural values and types of social behaviour and to retain only those which – in particular historical conditions – would increase their chances of survival and/or social advancement. The persistence of the pluriactive family throughout the modernisation phase provided a filter through which different options were considered and alternatively adopted and discarded. However, whereas before the war rural-industrial families had participated in the dominant Catholic culture primarily as 'recipients' – though admittedly as willing recipients because Catholic values strengthened the family unit and were opposed to economic and social change – after the war these families found themselves constrained by the Catholic establishment and actively participated in shaping new cultural attitudes. They forged an alliance with the Catholic unions and the left-wing of the newly-formed *partito popolare*, severing their links with the moderate Catholics, whose attitude to change was still one of total opposition.

Despite the attitude of the moderate Catholics, and their alliance with fascism in order to halt (or at least greatly slow down) change, the fascist period and the recession in particular greatly modified the local economy and society. From the point of view of pluriactive families the new changes were perceived as threatening, as they put paid to their aspirations to achieve self-sufficiency in agriculture. This time, however, their reaction was not so much to resist change but to weather the storm as best as they could, by relying on the support of all their members. In other words, as we saw in Chapter 4, they reverted to individualistic and family-related strategies while their attitude to political culture became increasingly instrumental. There was, for instance, neither vociferous opposition to fascism nor silent non-collaboration. Subsidies and practical help were never refused, and protests only took place when public works were judged to be insufficient or factories were threatened with closures.

The second post-war period, like the first, was a period of accelerated economic and social change, which presented pluriactive families with a renewed chance of achieving social advancement. It was also a period when Catholic culture re-emerged almost unscathed and came to dominate the western as well as the eastern areas. The reasons for the resilience of Catholic culture at a time when small landownership no longer constituted a viable proposition need to be addressed. What kind of change were the families now seeking and the Catholics proposing?

Let us look first at the province's political developments after the fall of fascism. In western Lombardy socialism resurfaced on a much weaker basis and was successfully replaced by political Catholicism, becoming confined to an urban environment. In eastern Lombardy Catholic culture survived almost unscathed, but only because it remained sensitive to the new needs and aspirations of local pluriactive families, as we shall now see.

Let us compare the electoral results of the pre-fascist period with those of the 1940s. Table 5.13 gives the electoral results in the relevant Lombard provinces before and after Fascism.

From Peasant to Entrepreneur

Table 5.13 Electoral Results in the Lombard Provinces of Como, Varese, Brescia and Bergamo, 1919, 1946, 1948 (Percentages)

| | 1919 | | | |
	Catholics	Socialists	Liberals	Others
Varese *circondario*	22.6	61.0	16.4	–
Como *circondario*	31.5	40.3	28.2	–
Lecco *circondario*	46.5	25.3	28.2	–
Province of Bergamo	64.4	14.7	20.9	–
Province of Brescia	45.5	23.7	18.5	12.3

| | 1946 | | | |
	Catholics	Socialists/ Communists	Liberals	Others
Province of Varese	43.2	50.6	1.9	4.3
Province of Como	47.1	44.7	3.3	4.9
Province of Bergamo	54.6	31.9	3.5	10.0
Province of Brescia	44.8	42.2	3.7	9.4

| | 1948 | | | |
	Catholics	Socialists/ Communists	Liberals/ Social/ Democrats	Others
Province of Varese	52.4	31.5	12.6	3.5
Province of Como	60.4	23.9	11.9	3.8
Province of Bergamo	73.6	14.3	8.7	3.4
Province of Brescia	61.4	28.4	7.5	2.7

Source: ISTAT Electoral Statistics. For the 1919 percentages by *circondari* the source was the Como Catholic newspaper, *Il Resegone*, 21–22 November 1919.

As Table 5.13 shows, in 1946 both the Catholic and the socialist votes regained their pre-war levels. Interestingly, while the Catholics made considerable inroads in the traditionally socialist area of Varese, the socialists did relatively better in the Catholic strongholds of eastern Lombardy. However, by 1948 it was clear that the Catholic vote of 1946 had formed a solid core of support upon which the Christian Democratic Party had been able to build up absolute majorities in all the provinces considered, while the socialist vote had proved a 'soft' political allegiance linked to the immediate post-war climate of renovation and reform. Thus in 1948 support for the socialists (including the communists) had returned to its pre-fascist level in the eastern provinces and it had 'collapsed' to roughly half that level in the Varese area. Here the socialists lost while the Catholics gained an absolute majority. These changes cannot be attributed to the fact that Varese was elevated to a provincial status in 1927, incorporating an area which had previously been part of the province of Milan, for the simple reason that many of the newly acquired councils had previously been under socialist administration.

We contend that these political changes were brought about by economic and social developments, namely the abandonment of agriculture during the fascist period accompanied by a renewed pressure to achieve upward mobility, this time in the industrial sector. As Table 5.14 shows, the decline of the agricultural sector was common to all the Lombard provinces where Christian Democracy triumphed.

Table 5.14 Active Population in Agriculture and Industry in the Lombard Provinces of Varese, Como, Bergamo and Brescia, 1921, 1936 and 1951 (Percentages)

	Agriculture			Industry		
	1921	1936	1951	1921	1936	1951
Province of Varese	28.9	15.2	6.0	57.9	68.9	75.2
Province of Como	40.5	23.9	13.6	51.0	58.8	66.1
Province of Bergamo	44.7	35.8	22.3	42.5	46.4	58.5
Province of Brescia	53.0	41.4	33.0	32.4	39.8	46.3

Sources: ISTAT Population Censuses.

The economic and social changes outlined above had the effect of weakening socialist culture while strengthening political Catholicism. Before arguing in favour of our hypothesis it is worth recalling that Trigilia, focusing his analysis on the two regions of Venetia and Emilia–Romagna, explained the re-emergence of the Catholic and socialist political subcultures after the Second World War on the basis of an ideological and traditional allegiance on the part of the local people linked to the persistence of a predominantly agricultural society.[16] It is clear that his explanation cannot be applied to Lombardy, where society had become predominantly industrial and where subcultural continuity with the pre-war period was not uniform. Indeed we suspect that even in Venetia, which was undoubtedly a much more agricultural region than Lombardy, this explanation does not hold, as the agricultural sector had come under severe strain during the fascist period and most of the newly-made small landowners of the 1920s found, just as in neighbouring Lombardy, that their new status was a dead end in terms of social advancement.[17]

We have to look somewhere else for an explanation. Obviously, there must be elements of continuity with the past amid the many changes, to explain the resilience and indeed the revival of Catholic culture after the war. The main element of continuity is the survival of the social form of the family. The pluriactive family, in fact, survived the period of intense social mobilisation/mobility after the First World War and continued to function as an economic unit. The recession of the late 1920s and early 1930s made small farmers economically non-viable and industrial workers precarious and underpaid, increasing the pressure on all family members to contribute to the family income.

Linked to the above is another important element of continuity, namely the pluriactive families' aspiration to achieve upward social mobility, though no longer in the primary sector. After the Second World War there was a renewed attempt on the part of local families to move from defensive to 'offensive' strategies, using as a lever the micro-entrepreneurial efforts of the recession period.

It is significant that, while Trigilia's explanation for the re-emergence of the Catholic subculture can be applied – at least on the surface – to Venetia but does not hold for Lombardy, our emphasis on other, less immediately discernible elements of continuity with the fascist and pre-fascist period provides an explanation that can be applied equally well to both regions.

In Venetia, as in Lombardy as we saw, in the 1930s many new small firms 'were set up ... sometimes leading a brief and difficult existence: they were nevertheless indicative of an entrepreneur-ship born out of micro-artisanal activities or of the effort made by local people to avoid unemployment in a period of recession by setting up on their own in traditional areas of production related to their professional skills.'[18]

The same link between the micro-entrepreneurship of the 1930s and that of the 1940s and 1950s that we found in Lombardy has been detected in Venetia:

In the fifteen years preceding and following the Second World War a surprisingly high level of activity characterised the small and medium-sized sector. It was a question of becoming entrepreneurs so as not to be unemployed. This was true in the 1910s, 1920s and 1930s and applies also to the period following the War ... it was then that small entrepreneurship acquired a new dynamism.[19]

In short, an agricultural sector on the way out (Lombardy) or in crisis (Venetia) and a widespread tendency towards micro-entrepreneurship before and after the Second World War had the effect of strengthening Catholic culture. This could hardly have been the result of a traditional and ideological allegiance to the subculture. As society had changed, so Catholic culture had had to adjust to the changes. It had done so in two ways.

First, it incorporated some of the moral values associated with the new entrepreneurial drive. Thus determination, risk-taking and ambition replaced submissiveness and resignation as the predominant motive forces for both individuals and families. Success and wealth came to be considered as reward for hard work and individual initiative, open to all those who would exert themselves. On the other hand, paternalism, charity and relief to the poor were delegated to the Church and did not form the basis of people's associationism. Alongside these 'new' values, some 'old' themes continued to strike a chord, though not for the same reasons. People still believed in the fundamental role of the family and in the duty of all its members to contribute to its well-being. Civil liberties were rejected, as they could bring a weakening of family values. There was a general respect for law and order, and for property, reflecting the local people's increasing access to land- and house-owning.

Secondly, at a more pragmatic and 'instrumental' level, the Catholics correctly interpreted and promptly supported the pluriactive families' pursuit of upward social mobility, aware that for many families this could now only be achieved through small-scale entrepreneurship, as opposed to small landownership. Catholic banks, for example, were encouraged to provide credit for local artisans and small industrialists; they were often instrumental in helping worker–peasant families to set up their own workshops. Incidentally, the same type of pressure was later applied to the communist subculture in the Emilia–Romagna region.

In this context the Christian Democratic Party's commitment to the creation and promotion of small businesses and the Communist Party's strategy of an alliance with the lower middle class must have had a reassuring effect on their respective constituencies. In Weiss's words:

> the PCI began at this time [1960s] to advance its anti-monopoly alliance strategy, championing small business interests nationally and assisting the self-employed in areas where it controlled local government resources. In parliamentary debates, the Communists' solicitude for small industry has at times seemed almost a parody of the Christian Democrat position ... the Communists' policy highlights the confidence and reality of social mobility that has characterised this stratum in Italian society over the post-war period.[20]

Rather surprisingly, Weiss rejects a similar relationship between socially-mobile strata and the pro-small-business policies of the Christian Democrats: 'government action on behalf of small enterprise is deducible not from the interests, needs or demands of particular socio-economic groupings but from the independent goals, ideals and interests of the ruling party.'[21] In the light of our research on Lombardy we would argue that the DC itself was heavily influenced by the social changes that were taking place in one of its subcultural strongholds. Indeed, the fact that the DC elaborated a programme of support for small business earlier than the PCI may simply have reflected the economic and social transformations they were witnessing in parts of northern Italy, in particular the non-viability of their long-standing policy aimed at creating a large class of small independent farmers.

This is indirectly confirmed, in our view, by looking at the regional distribution of State funds for small industry. Between 1953 and 1969, as Weiss herself reports, Lombard small firms were granted the highest amount, 162,635 million Lira, followed at a great distance by Emilia–Romagna (45,979 million), Piedmont (41,804), Venetia (37,068), and the Marches (15,110), and at much greater distance by the southern regions which were given 19,912 million Lira in all.[22] These sums were not granted in proportion to the number of firms already in existence: in 1962, in fact, artisanal firms amounted to 141,857 in Lombardy, 97,721 in Emilia–Romagna, 81,331 in Piedmont, 66,356 in Venetia, 33,143 in the Marches and 315,232 in the South.[23] In other words, Emilia–Romagna, with more than two-thirds of Lombardy's small firms, obtained less than a third of the funds allocated to

Lombardy; Piedmont, with more than half Lombardy's firms, was given a quarter of that region's funds; Venetia fared less badly, as it possessed less than half Lombardy's firms and it was given nearly a quarter of its funds; the Marches had almost a quarter of Lombardy's small firms and obtained less than a tenth of its funds; lastly, the South as a whole, with more than double the number of Lombardy's small firms, obtained just over 10 per cent of the funds allocated to that region.

Weiss overlooks the Lombard case because she is mainly concerned with showing that the Centre–North-East as a whole gained a larger share of State funding than the North-West or the South. Yet of all the Italian regions it was clearly Lombardy (and to a much lesser extent Venetia) which got the lion's share. Since their privileged position is not related to the then existing number of firms, it must be connected with the entrepreneurial drive of those two regions, actively supported by their Catholic subculture. The needs and demands of a social group on the move out of agriculture in traditional Catholic areas thus played a part in mobilising the DC and consequently the State in support of its aspirations.[24] Conversely, the poor showing of the southern region in terms of State funding for small businesses must be seen in relation to the absence of a socially-driven entrepreneurial activity outside farming. We cannot agree with Weiss that State strategies and 'vision' count but families' and communities' do not.

To conclude, at the root of Catholic predominance in the province of Como before and after the fascist period lies a successful reversal of the process of proletarianisation of peasant families. In the nineteenth and early twentieth centuries it was the silk industry which effectively stopped this process, at a time when it was well in advance elsewhere. Social promotion may already have represented the dominant aspiration of rural/industrial families, but on the whole social immobility was seen as a safer alternative to attempting change. Upward social mobility was later tried after the First World War, and in the short term it was successful. The recession of the late 1920s and 1930s, however, put paid to the local families' aspirations of achieving self-sufficiency in agriculture. The new wave of industrialisation opened up new opportunities; members of peasant–worker families found employment as factory workers, but resented becoming increasingly proletarianised. From the 1940s onwards it was the main protagonists of the new industrialisation – artisans and small industrialists, even homeworkers – who fought against the prospect of giving up their cherished 'independence'; once again they turned to political Catholicism, which they saw as their best ally.

There are now signs that the subcultures – both Catholic and communist – are weakening. Yet the family in Italy seems to have found renewed vitality and resilience.[25] If this were the case we would have to conclude that the social form of the family, as described and defined in this book, has outlived not only the economic structure – intermediate between agriculture and industry – which created it in the first place, but also the cultural framework which accompanied its creation. However tempting this analysis might be, there is no real evidence that the declining subcultures are losing ground to pragmatic, neo-liberal values and political institutions. Indeed in the Catholic areas the old subculture may simply be replaced by a new and up-to-date version of itself, as the recent emergence of the so-called *Leghe* in Lombardy and other northern regions points to.

The *Leghe* are regionally-based loose political organisations which have borrowed and revived the traditional subcultural role of defenders of the local identity and autonomy against the central State (and southern immigrants) but have also taken on the representation of the interests of the entrepreneurial class. The *Leghe* have obtained very good results in the local and regional elections. The *Lega Lombarda*, for example, triumphed at the administrative elections of May 1990, mainly at the expense of the Christian Democrats – it gained 20 per cent of the overall regional votes, with particularly good results in the 'white' provinces of Como (28 per cent), Bergamo (26 per cent) and Brescia (25 per cent).[26] The *Lega* campaigned on a platform which combined a generic protest against the party system and a no-less generic demand for a federal State with very specific reforms directly supportive of local entrepreneurship. Among these were the privatisation of public services, fewer taxes, particularly for businesses, and the opening of all public offices in the afternoon (a well-known sore point for private enterprise).[27] The *Leghe's* curious mixture of Thatcherism and regionalism/parochialism can only be understood with reference to an entrepreneurial but also closely communitarian economy and society.

The *Leghe* may well turn out to be a passing phenomenon, born out of a generic protest against State inefficiency and racial prejudice. Were they to overcome the DC party in Lombardy and Venetia, however, we would have to conclude that, as a specific form of capitalist development, localised industrial communities operate best in a subcultural context and indeed strive to perpetuate their specificity – even parochialism – resisting complete secularisation.[28]

Notes

1. INEA, *La distribuzione della proprietà fondiaria in Italia*: Lombardia, ed. G. Medici, Rome 1951, p. XIII.

2. Ibid., pp. XV–XVI.

3. ISTAT 1921 and 1936 Population Censuses.

4. See G. Sapelli (ed.), *La classe operaia durante il fascismo*, Annali della Fondazione G. Feltrinelli, XX, Milan, 1981. Also A. Cento Bull, 'Appunti per un'analisi della famiglia operaia e contadina sotto il fascismo', *Studi e Ricerche di Storia Contemporanea*, no.16, Bergamo 1981.

5. R. Griglia (ed.), *La Grande Brianza*, Milan 1978, p. 369.

6. ISTAT 1936 Population Census.

7. Ibid.

8. Archivio di Stato di Como, Fondo Prefettura-Gabinetto, b.6, Relazione dei Carabinieri, 23 August 1932.

9. Atti della Commissione Parlamentare d'Inchiesta sulla disoccupazione, Vol.III, Tomo 1, Camera dei Deputati, Rome 1953, p. 426.

10. F. Della Peruta, R. Leydi and A. Stella, *Mondo popolare in Lombardia. Milano e il suo territorio*, Milan 1985, pp. 538–9.

11. S. Brusco, 'Small Firms and Industrial Districts in Italy', in D. Keeble and E. Wever (eds), *New Firms and Regional Development in Europe*, London 1986, pp. 188–9.

12. Della Peruta *et al.*, *Mondo popolare in Lombardia*, p. 539.

13. M. Pitt, J. Szarka and A. Bull, 'Executive Characteristics, Strategic Choices and Small Firm Development: A Three-Country Study of Small Textile and Clothing Firms', *International Small Business Journal*, vol.9, no.3, April–June 1991, pp. 20–2.

14. The survey was carried out in 1989 as part of a wider research project on textile and clothing small-firm communities in Italy, France and Great Britain. The project was financed by the European Commission. The main research tool was a postal questionnaire, combined with a

limited number of follow-up interviews, both in-company and by phone. The data utilised in this chapter, unless otherwise stated, are original unpublished material.

15. The percentages quoted do not add up to one hundred because informants were told that their replies were not mutually exclusive. In other words, we accepted that someone might wish to accord a degree of preference to his or her own relatives as well as to relatives of colleagues and employees.

16. C. Trigilia, *Grandi partiti e piccole imprese:Comunisti e democristiani nelle regioni a economia diffusa*, Bologna 1986, p. 64.

17. E. Brunetta, 'Dalla Grande Guerra alla Repubblica', in *Storia d'Italia. Le Regioni dall'Unità a oggi. Il Veneto*, ed. S. Lanaro, Turin 1984, pp. 959–62.

18. G. Roverato 'La terza regione industriale', in *Storia d'Italia. Il Veneto*, p. 199.

19. Ibid., p. 203.

20. L.Weiss, *Creating Capitalism. The State and Small Business since 1945*, Oxford 1988, pp. 49–50.

21. Ibid., p. 125.

22. Ibid., p. 75.

23. G. Lasorsa, *L'Artigianato in Italia*, Rome, Ministero dell'Industria e del Commercio, Direzione Generale dell'Artigianato e delle piccole industrie, 1963, p. 106.

24. Not to mention the Church. According to Roverato parish priests in Venetian rural villages were often instrumental in promoting local industrial initiatives. They did this to find an alternative to a declining agricultural sector and above all to prevent young people from emigrating to the towns and cities, which would have led to a disruption of local society. Roverato, 'La terza regione industriale', in *Storia d'Italia. Il Veneto*, p. 208.

25. P.Ginsborg, *A History of Contemporary Italy. Society and Politics 1943–1988*, pp. 412–16.

26. *Corriere della Sera*, 8–5–1990.

27. Interviews with leaders of the *Lega Lombarda* and comments on their political platform in *Panorama*, 20–5–90, 3–6–90, 17–6–90, 1–7–90, 22–7–90.

28. The general political elections of April 1992 gave further boost to the lega lombarda, particularly in the "white" provinces of Varese, Como, Bergamo and Brescia. Some of the best results were obtained in the areas forming industrial districts. See A. Cento Bull, 'The *Lega Lombarda*: a new political subculture for Lombardy's localised industries' in *The Italianist*, No 12, 1992

6
Beyond Silk: Italy's Model of Diffused Industrialisation

6.1 Small Firms as an Independent Form of Industrial Organisation

In the last chapter we made two unsubstantiated claims, namely that it is futile and unproductive to divide Como's small firms into separate sectors and subsectors and that diffused industrialisation, born out of a specific *social* form, now also stands for a distinct – some would say unique – economic form. The full implications of the existence of overlapping economic activities and of specific industrial and organisational traits will now be addressed, in the context of recent theories on *industrial districts*.

The economist Alfred Marshall was the first to coin the term 'industrial district', by which he meant 'a concentration of large numbers of small businesses of a similar kind in the same locality'.[1] Different districts have had different origins, primarily due to particular physical conditions. However, according to Marshall, they all have a few characteristics in common, namely the concentration and easy availability of skilled labour, the use of highly specialised machinery, the constant spread of innovation and the combination of social and economic forces. The viability of industrial districts was attributed by Marshall to the presence of external economies and to an unspecified 'industrial atmosphere' which guaranteed that vital information and innovation was shared by all.

Rediscovering and discussing Marshall on the basis of his own empirical observation of Italy's small business communities, Becattini emphasised some years ago that the industrial district itself, rather than the individual firm or the industrial sector, should constitute the unit of analysis.[2] Any analysis of industrial districts must overcome the traditional division between economic sectors (primary, secondary, tertiary) and subsectors (textiles, metalworking, shoemaking, etc.). Each district does indeed possess a 'core' manufacturing industry, be it textiles, furniture-making or light engineering. However, it is also characterised by the existence of a vertical value-chain which may extend on the one hand to the making of the machinery needed at each stage of the production process and on the other to wholesalers, trade intermediaries and marketing agencies.

Since then, a few up-to-date definitions of the industrial district phenomenon have been put forward, some of them more of an operational type, others of a more theoretical nature.

Brusco and Sabel described small firms in an industrial district as producing for a national and international market, being connected by subcontracting links yet operating in a highly competitive environment.[3] Collaboration also plays an important part, though mainly among firms which carry out different jobs, as well as within each firm between management and the most skilled workers. Collaboration of this kind is highly conducive to constant innovation and the acquisition of skill, through a process of learning-by-doing.

Garofoli chose to coin a new term, that of 'system-areas', each containing a high number of small firms producing the same goods or specialising in different stages of the production process, thus complementing each other.[4] A marked division of labour characterises these latter firms, while a high level of competition exists between firms which produce the same goods or are involved in the same phase of production. In both cases innovation spreads rapidly, in a chain fashion between firms linked vertically (clients, suppliers, subcontractors), or simply by imitation between horizontal firms (competitors). The result is that when a technical innovation is introduced in one firm it soon becomes common knowledge in the district, to the benefit of all local producers.[5]

More recently, Becattini defined an industrial district as 'a form of industrial organization and, at the same time, a local community, which results from the interplay between a population of persons living and working in a certain geographical area and a population of small and medium sized firms belonging to a certain industrial branch (e.g. textiles, shoes, furniture etc.)'.[6] What distinguishes a district from any other industrial area is 'the existence of a specialised network for selling its products to the final markets and an "image" of the same district, such as to be relevant for the choices of the professional agents in the field'.[7]

The definitions listed above do not necessarily complement

each other, as the theory is still far from constituting a coherent body. Nevertheless, there are sufficient elements in the literature on industrial districts to indicate that they form an independent, almost unique form of industrial organisation which can rival large firms in the international markets for quality of products and speed and efficiency of production as well as technical innovation.

Do Como small firms fit the sophisticated 'model' put forward by the theorists? The answer is that by and large they do. Although not all firms in the province of Como operate in an industrial district, those which do account for a relevant proportion of the province's economy. Each of the province's three main towns is an industrial centre which specialises in a particular industrial branch: if Como is renowned for silk manufacturing, Lecco is a well-known metalworking centre and Cantù a carpenters' town. Each has a satellite-area made up of its immediate neighbouring villages, which gravitate towards their own centre's main industrial activity. Cantù has ten such villages; together they account for 59 per cent of the province's woodworking and furniture-making firms and for 69 per cent of their employees. Lecco has eleven; their degree of specialisation is less striking, mainly because metalworking has now become the province's most important industry, and has expanded in all its areas. Nevertheless, Lecco and its satellite villages account for 24 per cent of the province's metalworking firms and 33 per cent of their employees. Como has roughly 17–18 neighbouring textile villages: they account for 41 per cent of the province's textile firms and 50 per cent of their employees. In addition, the province contains two other textile areas, one which specialises in the manufacturing of velvet/corduroy and the other in fabrics for nets and curtains. Together, the Como district and these two subdistricts account for virtually all the province's textile industry. In short, manufacturing in this province is highly concentrated in geographical terms but not in industrial or financial terms. It is also highly specialised: textiles means mainly silk; woodworking means furniture-making; metalworking means mainly metal-ware and the making of metal accessories as well as foundries. A series of industrial districts and subdistricts succeed each other from north to south and from east to west, particularly in the hilly parts of the province. Most of these districts are characterised by a marked division of labour between firms, constant innovation, high levels of investment and the use of skilled labour.

The results are very positive. The silk industry, for example, exported between 50 per cent and 70 per cent of its production throughout the 1980s, accounting for nearly 10 per cent of the total surplus made by Italy's textiles-clothing sector.[8] It has come to dominate the lucrative American market where, as a local industrialist put it, 'we dictate prices and fashion'. It has developed a particularly efficient marketing structure, thanks to the emergence of the so-called 'Converters' (see below). 'The province of Como is a small Japan' was how the Italian newspaper *La Repubblica* summarised the province's industrial success in textiles.[9]

The furniture industry is not far behind. It started, as we saw, at the beginning of the century as an artisanal industry, a characteristic it gradually lost by developing a modern industrial structure. What did not change was the size of firms: in 1981 the average number of employees per firm was 4.8. Again, high levels of investment, innovation, skilled labour and a specialised selling network (mainly through 'permanent' fairs and exhibitions) are the characteristics of this export-oriented industry.

The mechanical industry, in and around the town of Lecco, though lacking one of the features of an industrial district – inter-firm and intersectorial links are not well developed there as they are at Como or Cantù[10] – is nonetheless another local agglomeration of specialist small firms which are both export-oriented and highly-capitalised.

Indeed, the whole northern strip of the Pre-Alps from Piedmont through Lombardy to Venetia can be decribed as a series of local agglomerations of small firms, whose present-day characteristics appear to be an efficient and competitive organisation of production. Wool textiles at Biella, light engineering at Bergamo, steel (Brescia), arms (Gardone Val Trompia), domestic appliances (Lumezzane), tights and stockings, lighting (Castel Goffredo), ski boots (Montebelluna) are just some further examples of competitive industries whose products are well-known both within and outside Italy.

Within each of the above districts manufacturing remains the 'core' activity yet, as Becattini rightly stressed, their function and success cannot be properly understood if the full range of economic activities they carry out is not taken into consideration. We can take the Como silk district as an example.[11]

The Como silk district is made up of the town of Como and roughly 17–18 villages situated within a ten-kilometre radius of the town itself. In 1981 it comprised just over 500 enterprises and 15,000 employees in textiles manufacturing. The degree of specialisation in textiles is high though not exclusive, textiles manufacturing accounting for 20 per cent of the total number of local firms and 50 per cent of the total industrial workforce. On the other hand, the degree of specialisation in silk manufacturing of the district within Italy is extremely high: Como makes up virtually the whole of Italy's silk industry. Thus an industry which accounts for a tenth of Italy's textile-clothing sector is concentrated in an area covering roughly one hundred and thirty square kilometres and measuring roughly eight kilometres by seventeen. Geographic concentration, such as pertains to an industrial district, does not mean industrial concentration: Como firms typically employ between ten and one hundred employees, with only a handful with more than five hundred (but still less than 1,000). Population within the district amounted in 1981 to 150,000.

The 'core' manufacturing activity is silk fabrics. However, a whole series of subsidiary activities gravitate around this core industry, many of which are not strictly manufacturing activities: fashion design, wholesaling and retailing of cloths manufactured within the district, services to industry, such as marketing and consultancy, credit and financing, etc.; also fairs and exhibitions, fashion shows, export centres. Other centres offer a variety of services and advice to local textile firms. The Centro Volta, for example, promotes pure and applied research, while the Centro Tessile at present is concentrating its efforts on encouraging firms to introduce computerised systems. Applied, textile-related technology is taught in local schools and colleges. The launch of a new university faculty offering courses in textile engineering is currently being discussed. In addition, the Chamber of Commerce, the local industrialists' association, the textile trade unions and local Government institutions are all interested parties in catering for the needs of the textile industry and in sustaining economic growth.

The degree of firm specialisation is extremely high, and local firms can be easily grouped according to their function. The main groups of specialised firms are:

(1) Designers (*Disegnatori*). These create the patterns which are then reproduced on the cloth either at the loom or at the printing stage.

(2) Weavers (*Greggisti*). These make the standard cloth, either independently or acting as subcontractors to the *vertical* firms or the *converters* (see below). They can, in turn, contract out work to other weaving firms. Some weaving firms also manufacture silk ties, handkerchiefs and headscarves which, together with shirts and blouses, are Como's only finished products.

(3) 'Ennobling' firms, i.e. finishing, printing and dyeing firms (*Tintostampatori*). These can specialise in just one, two or all three of the above activities. They are always subcontractors to the *vertical* firms and the *converters*.

In turn, like the weavers, they can contract out work to other similar specialist firms. This type of firms tend to possess the newest machinery and are capable of 'ennobling' any type of fibre or cloth, from silk to cotton, from wool to mixed or man-made fibres. They rely on local artistic designers for sophisticated and fashionable patterns.

(4) Vertical firms (*Imprese terminali*). These are integrated, medium-to-large firms which carry out all the different operations present in the district. They buy the fabrics, undertake the most sophisticated weaving work (contracting out the more routine work to weaving firms), print and dye the cloth (but also make use of local specialist firms) and, lastly, market the final product.

(5) Wholesalers/Co-ordinators (*Converters*). These are commercial operators/wholesalers/merchants. They receive orders on the basis of their own pattern-books, and organise the production chain. They buy the fibres and contract out work to local weavers, dyers and printers. Their products are sold both nationally and internationally. These 'merchants' generally know markets and fashion trends well, and ensure local production responds quickly to consumer demands and keeps ahead of its competitors.

The industrial structure of the Como textile district can be represented graphically as follows:

Figure 6.1 Industrial Structure of the Como Textile District

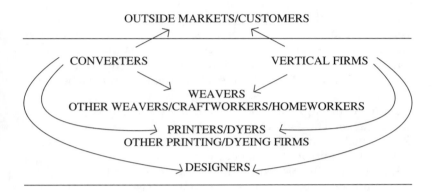

The above graphic shows that Como does indeed possess, as Becattini suggested, a specialised network for selling local production to external markets. Such a network is made up of both vertical firms and converters. The links between these firms and all the other economic actors operating in the district are provided by subcontracting arrangements. These ensure that a vertical value-chain is achieved and that the various activities come together into a loose but also smooth and efficient structure, known locally as the *filiera*. It is thanks to the existence of the *filiera* that technical innovations and new designs spread quickly throughout the district and that a high rate of investment *per firm* is achieved. Being highly specialised, each firm tends to use only a limited, though sophisticated, stock of machinery, and can afford to renovate it at regular intervals. In 1984 alone, for example, local textile firms invested fifty billion Lira in new machinery while another ten billion were spent on design and researching new fabrics. Investment was made not only by the larger firms, but also by the hundreds of small specialist firms which make up the district.

In terms of future trends, the forecast is for a further loss of employees in the more traditional sectors, including textiles, and for a shift towards the tertiary sector. Having said this, the province of Como, and indeed Lombardy as a whole, has shown that it is not prepared to let the more mature sectors go and be replaced by the services industry. In other words, the increase in the services sector does not automatically mean that the weight of the manufacturing sector will substantially decrease, at least in terms of wealth-creation. The entrepreneurial and industrial vocation of the Lombard region – sometimes known as industrial conservatism – has probably been an important human and cultural factor behind the endurance and tenacity of its traditional industrial sectors, such as textiles and particularly silk, in these difficult times.

Seen in this light, Como's small businesses take on a new significance. They have come to constitute a specific *economic* form which encompasses the local community. The function of the family is mirrored in that of the community.

Like the family, the community does not simply represent a socio-cultural referent, but an economic quasi-organisation that can be described and analysed in its own right. The dynamism of the family depends on the various members' pooling skills and resources; similarly, the dynamism and growth of the district depends on the success of individual firms which are part of it, in so far as these are able to contribute to each other's competitiveness. Thus local firms, despite being small, achieve a *de facto* complementarity and interdependence. As the family, in its function as an entrepreneurial unit, blurs and overcomes occupational divisions and social statuses, so the community as a quasi-organisation stretches across different economic activities.

The literature on industrial districts has, for some time now, crossed paths with the literature on the Third Italy. In the 1960s and 1970s, in fact, entire regions of Italy were able to industrialise, following the creation of a myriad of new small and family-run firms in traditional manufacturing sectors, particularly textiles and clothing, shoes and leather goods, woodworking and furniture making as well as light engineering.[12] The regions affected – collectively named by Bagnasco the *Third Italy* to distinguish them from both the north-western industrial triangle and the underdeveloped southern areas – were Venetia, Emilia-Romagna, Tuscany, the Marches and Umbria. While Venetia, like northern Lombardy and other sub-Alpine areas, shares a similar economic background, having been the site of the earlier, silk-related industrialisation, the other regions present a different economic profile, having remained in some cases predominantly agricultural until very recent times. In the next two sections we will compare the older diffused industrialisation of the sub-Alpine region with that of central Italy and review the many, often contrasting, interpretations of the Third Italy phenomenon in the light of our own findings.

6.2 The 'Italian Model'. Current Debates on its Origins and Characteristics

There does not seem to be a common explanation of the origins of areas of diffused entrepreneurship. Consequently, there is no agreement as to how they develop and whether they can be recreated in different environments, or even simply sustained and strengthened in their existing ones. The literature on this topic is vast – we will therefore only review the main interpretations, which can be broadly grouped into three categories, the socio-historical, the economic and the political.

Bagnasco and especially Paci identified the Third Italy with a common rural origin; these were all sharecropping areas, based on extended peasant families used to heavy working routines and an internal division of labour.[13] Such families functioned almost like entrepreneurial, self-sufficient units and found it easier, when the sharecropping system disintegrated in the 1950s and 1960s, to move into the industrial sector as independent producers (artisans and small-scale entrepreneurs), rather than as wage-earners.

Criticisms of Paci's interpretation have come from various sources. Italian researchers have pointed out that many new entrepreneurs in the Third Italy were of urban, rather than rural origins, and in most cases had acquired their experience by previously working as employees in local factories.[14] This debate seems to have gradually lost steam, since it is possible that the relationship between sharecropping and entrepreneurship was a two-step one, with the sharecropper gaining some experience as a wage-earner before setting up on his own. Brusco claimed that this relationship is a complex one and 'passes through a sedimentation of managerial competence within the whole social texture'.[15] Even more conclusively, Bagnasco pointed out, with reference to Tuscany, that in the 1950s 70 per cent of the population were employed in agriculture, while the corresponding figure for the 1980s was 10 per cent. Since immigration to the region during that period had been fairly limited, it must be concluded that today's social groups originate from the rural 'reservoir'.[16]

In common with the socio-historical interpretation, the economic interpretation of the revival of small firms has been considerably influenced by the Italian experience, though for different reasons. In the 1970s Italy went through a process of industrial decentralisation, due to the high costs and rigidity of the labour force in the larger firms. Accordingly the economic literature argues that the high number of small firms is mainly the outcome of new management strategies and the wider use of subcontractors on the part of large firms. Brusco sees this explanation as applicable to some recently formed areas of diffused industrialisation, such as CastelGoffredo, Reggio Emilia and Modena.[17] Basing their observations on empirical evidence gathered at Prato (Tuscany), Lorenzoni and Ornati have also argued that a large firm, by following a strategy of de-integration, encourages the formation of smaller firms which, though independent, are increasingly drawn together till they form interlocking networks.[18]

The political interpretation, often mingled with the sociological one, stresses the role of political 'subcultures' and institutions in sustaining the formation of closely-knit industrial communities. In this context Trigilia sees little difference between regions with a predominantly Catholic (white) subculture and regions with a predominantly communist (red) one.[19] Whatever the political 'credo' of a region, the fact that the local community subscribed to common ideological/religious beliefs led to the prevalence of solidarity and co-operation within it and to a common identity *vis-à-vis* the world outside. However, a few important differences were registered between red and white areas, in so far as in the former local political institutions, including the Communist Party, the trade unions and the local councils, were found to be more actively involved in supporting economic development. This was partly attributed by Trigilia to historical traditions of respectively high and low levels of political participation in red and white regions. Brusco also maintained that local authorities in the red region of Emilia–Romagna were more efficient than those in the white region of Venetia. Since, however, small-firm agglomerations can be found in both areas, he concluded that 'basic forces, engrafted into the whole social structure ... have given rise to the growth of the districts', thus reverting to a sociological interpretation.[20]

Nanetti put forward the hypothesis that the success of small firms in Italy was due in no small part to the active involvement of local political institutions, especially after the establishment of the regions as autonomous administrative entities in 1970. Laws 382 of 1975 and 616 of 1977 'institutionalised the regions as real centres of policy-making'.[21] Since then, they have played an important role as providers of 'advance services to industry to contain the costs of innovation and restructuring of productive capacity and to secure new markets'.[22]

Weiss rejected these interpretations, arguing that central Government played a much bigger role in promoting small-business development than is generally acknowledged. The Christian Democratic Party, in particular, had a strong ideological commitment to small entrepreneurs and the self-employed, and introduced supportive legislation as well as providing economic incentives.[23]

The same divergent opinions which are held with respect to the origins of the Third Italy and of industrial districts are also to be found regarding their characteristics and functions. The 'flexible specialisation' theory, in particular, has given rise to a heated debate on the economic performance and competitiveness of localised industrial systems. The debate can be briefly summarised.

Flexible specialisation refers to 'the manufacture of specialized goods using flexible machinery and skilled labour in contrast to the mass production of standardized goods using special-purpose equipment and unskilled workers'.[24] The recent industrialisation of the Third Italy was singled out by Piore and Sabel as an example of flexible specialisation. Sabel has argued that there is now a gradual convergence of both large firms and industrial districts towards similar organisational forms. We are witnessing, according to this theory, the unfolding of a new historical-economic phase which will mark the end of mass production and the birth or at least the readjustment of political institutions to cope with the new forms of capitalist development.

The theory is imaginative and exciting, as well as provocative. It produces, however, a uniform category under which all areas of small-scale development are subsumed, irrespective of their differences. Sabel admits that these differences can be very substantial, and that not all industrial districts have proceeded or are ever likely to proceed along the path that leads to flexible specialisation, but he does not probe the issue. Yet it is a crucial one, for the suspicions and misconceptions that the flexible specialisation theory has created are largely due to what appears an unjustifiable glorification of sweatshop conditions of work and pay.[25] It could be argued, along the line of Marshall's and Becattini's definitions, that many areas of localised production simply do not conform to the model and should not be confused with it. Amin's research on the shoe industry in Naples and Blim's research on the same sector in the Marches have shown very clearly that they are a world apart from the sophisticated industrial areas referred to by Piore and Sabel.[26]

Where does all this leave us? Confusion seems to reign. Matters are not made easier by the fact that the successful development of the Third Italy is either branded as the incarnation of an egalitarian enterprising society of craft-producers or condemned as just another version of Italy's submerged economy and illegal labour exploitation. There are those who advocate exporting this phenomenon to both developing and developed countries, and those who reject what they see at worst as a return to ninenteenth-century work conditions and at best as a short-lived phenomenon due largely to a contingent favourable demand.

We believe that our research on the Comasco can contribute both to clarify the issues involved, and to a better understanding of the origins of small-scale industrialisation and its present-day characteristics. For these reasons we will now reassess the debate so far in the light of our own findings.

6.3 A Reassessment of Current Theories: The Social Variables of Small-Business Performance

There are two main issues at stake concerning Italy's small-scale industrialisation. The first is about its origins, both in terms of historical roots and in terms of periodisation. The second issue is about the economic and social characteristics of this type of industrialisation today, and its degree of competitiveness in the world markets.

With regard to the first issue, our research on the Brianza emphasises the social roots of small-scale industrialisation, and thus has points of contact with Paci's and, more recently, with Blim's interpretations. The main difference seems to be one of periodisation; our research suggests that the recent 'new wave' of industrialisation, typified by the Third Italy, does in fact follow a pattern that was fairly common for whole areas of northern Italy during the earlier phases of industrialisation, but which has, to some extent, remained obscured by the conviction that, on the one hand, textiles and small-scale manufacturing were necessarily indications of backward forms of industrial production, and on the other, by the excessive attention given to big industry as an index of industrial progress. In reality it seems that the process of transition from agricultural work to manufacturing on a small scale has been a constant source of dynamism in certain areas and in certain conditions for most of this century.

In this context explanations of the Third Italy that go back only a few decades – Weiss's, for example, or Nanetti's – do not appear to grasp the long-term significance of the persistence of the family economy, first as a peasant or peasant–worker unit, later as a worker–peasant and then an entrepreneurial unit.

Nevertheless, despite the obvious points of contact between our findings and existing 'sociological' interpretations of the Third Italy, the social form we have identified does not coincide with that brought to light by Paci and Blim. This may have important implications for the debate on the second issue, i.e. on the economic characteristics of small-scale industrialisation.

In particular, it seems to us that the social form we described in this book is associated with well-established and technologically advanced areas of small-scale production, while Blim's entrepreneurs operate in a weakly competitive environment. We have already pointed out that the whole sub-Alpine strip from Piedmont to Venetia can be described as a series of local agglomerations of small firms which are efficient, competitive and innovative. Similar small-scale industrial agglomerations exist in Emilia–Romagna and Tuscany. They can also be found further South, in Umbria and the Marches; here, however, small-scale industries appear generally of a less competitive type. In the Marches, as Blim's research shows, firms are generally under-capitalised, employ largely unskilled labour, depend on outside buyers for orders (rather than promoting their products through specialist channels) and are currently at risk of entering a phase of de-industrialisation.[27]

How do we reconcile these two types of industry, the forward-looking, highly capitalised 'industrial district' type and the precarious, under-capitalised, labour-exploiting version? Can industrial competitiveness, as well as entrepreneurship, be linked to social variables? And in what ways does the social form prevalent in Northern Lombardy differ from that of the Marches? These are important questions and need to be addressed in some detail.

It could be argued, of course, that the two versions of small-scale industrialisation represent two different stages of development – the Marches and Umbria were the last to join in the industrial process, and they may need more time to become more efficient. Time, in particular, for the second, better-trained and more sophisticated generation of entrepreneurs to take over from the self-made, poorly skilled generation of founders. There is some truth in this, as the Como development outlined in the previous sections implies.

Nevertheless, a reassessment of the transition from agriculture to industry in the two areas will show some socio-historical differences which may help explain their subsequent development.

In the Pre-Alps the protagonist of small-scale industrialisation was the peasant family, whose members were able to engage in non-agricultural activities while continuing to live on and to derive some income from the land. We have defined this family in the course of this book as a peasant-worker family. From Paci's description of the transition from peasant to entrepreneur in the Marches one would be tempted to conclude that the same type of family was at work there. Yet this may well not be the case.

Paci's analysis of the transition from sharecroppers to small entrepreneurs in the Marches is worth recalling here. Paci identifies the following factors in, and steps towards, diffused entrepreneurship connected with the sharecropping system in the Marches region:

(1) Sharecropping households possessed some capital which remained 'frozen' in the form of agricultural tools and cattle until the 1950s and 1960s, when the sharecropping system broke down.

(2) Each household made a collective effort to save and gain social promotion, under the authority and direction of its male head.

(3) Being a multiple family, it could release a few members from agricultural work and send them to earn a wage in industry

without losing its ties with the land.

(4) Once the sharecropping family acquired a plot of land, it discovered that it could not make a living out of it through capitalist farming. The family was thus 'expelled' from the primary sector.

(5) The family was then drawn towards the industrial sector, where some of its members had already found employment.

(6) The expertise gained by those members of the household employed in industry was shared with the other members, whose labour was made use of, regardless of sex and age. The entire household was transformed into an entrepreneurial unit.

It is easy to detect, in Paci's description, the transformation of the sharecropping family from a purely farming unit to a peasant–worker and then a worker–peasant household. The similarities with the Brianza's process of development are no doubt striking, but so too are the differences, if one observes more clearly the relationship between families and land – encompassing that between town and country – in the two areas, and the families' changing profile under the impact of growing involvement with non-agricultural occupations, as well as the duration of the transition itself.

Let us start with the last aspect, i.e. with the time factor. In the Marches steps (3), (4), (5) and (6) above appear to have been accomplished in just two or three decades. Once the sharecropping system broke down, it all happened very quickly, all to the credit of the entrepreneurial drive of a social group which until the 1950s had had very little knowledge of or contact with industrial work. In Brianza, by contrast, step (3) had started as early as the late eighteenth century, and had extended to the rest of the region by the middle of the nineteenth century, at least as far as female members of the family were concerned. For men the process started in the late nineteenth century, accelerated during the fascist period, and became widespread in the 1940s and 1950s. Step (6) was started in a few areas in the nineteenth century, attempted on a larger scale in the fascist period, and resumed and completed in the 1950s and 1960s. Each step, in other words, covered a period varying from a minimum of forty years (entrepreneurship) to a maximum of one hundred and fifty (peasant–worker to worker–peasant).

In addition, in Brianza each step or phase tended to include an early period of 'incubation', during which the new form would make its appearance but remain marginal compared to the dominant social mode, a middle stage of 'full emersion' in which the change would become widespread but its significance would not be clearly perceived at the cultural–political level, and a final stage of 'consolidation', marking the resilience of the phenomenon and a general understanding of its implications and involving some form of institutionalised response to it.

Thus, for example, the transition from peasant-worker to worker-peasant made its appearance in Brianza in the late-nineteenth century, particularly in the Varesotto and the area around Cantù, but remained marginal *vis-à-vis* the dominant social mode of the province (peasant–worker), and was at the time perceived as a process of proletarianisation. The transition was accelerated throughout the province during the fascist period, yet at the cultural-political level its implications were not clearly understood, as both the local population and the fascist authorities still tended to regard farming as a viable economic activity. By the end of the Second World War most families were now worker-peasant and they seemed at last to have the full measure of the transition they had experienced: they knew that it could either lead to proletarianisation proper or be exploited to achieve economic independence and a higher social status. Politically, Christian Democracy institutionalised their aspirations with its pro-small-business policies.

Similarly, entrepreneurship born out of the worker–peasant family form started in the nineteenth century (Cantù), was more widely attempted in the fascist period, when it was perceived as yet another expression of pluriactivity, and was finally followed up with cultural 'vision' and political support in the 1950s and 1960s.

The existence of an initial 'phasing-in' period and a final consolidation stage within each of the steps that led to small-scale entrepreneurship in Brianza should not be underestimated. It means that economic development and social and cultural change, though proceeding at uneven paces, were able to find their own ways to harmonise and support each other. There was time for each change to 'sink in' to the local society, to shape it as well as be shaped by it. The same cannot be said of the Marches, where the rise of small-scale industry was fast and even successful; but its impact on society and culture appears to have been only superficial: thus social aspirations and cultural values can at times be supportive of economic development, yet equally they can obstruct it.

The second difference between the two areas concerns the relationship between families and land, and town and country. The North-Italian peasant–worker (later worker–peasant) family typically combined rural and industrial work, and gradually abandoned the former for the latter without moving residence – it industrialised, so to speak, on the spot. This meant that the land it rented or possessed was instrumental to entrepreneurial activity in at least three ways: (i) it helped to keep down consumption costs; (ii) it could be used as security to raise loans; and (iii) it provided both living and work premises. What we witness, therefore, is a gradual transformation of the family into an entrepreneurial unit and of the plot of land into an industrial enterprise. The end result is what is known as 'urbanised' or 'industrialised' countryside, which means that there is a continuum, rather than a neat division, between urban and rural settlements. There can be no going back to full-time farming or landownership because the land is too fragmented; this is true even to the extent that the remaining farms, at least in northern Lombardy, are themselves small enterprises in terms of size, which do well because they are highly specialised and capitalised.

What we have said explains why local families are renowned for investing heavily into their business. The logic of the family requires that it provide for all its members and for future generations. The disappearance of farming as an alternative and the possibility of solving housing needs – particularly in the early stages of the transition to entrepreneurship – by renovating or even totally rebuilding, maybe as a block of flats, the old farmhouse, means that the family firm is perceived as the best outlet for the reinvestment of profits.

A somewhat different picture is presented to us by Blim; the peasant family he has observed in the Marches typically moved from the countryside to the towns after an initial period of combining farming with industrial work. Paci also makes reference to this pattern of migration from the rural to the urban areas, though he specifies that it often took place in two stages. First the family acquired a small plot of land – much smaller than the one they had farmed as sharecroppers – just outside a town with a developing industrial and commercial sector and took up residence there. The land would then be cultivated for the family's own consumption needs while some members would take up work in a factory or artisanal workshop in the town (worker–peasant stage). Later the family moved to the town itself to set up its own firm. The abandonment of farming thus seems to have been accompanied by the abandonment of the land itself and of the peasant family's native place, in contrast to the Lombard experience.[28] Once in town, the new entrepreneurial family found itself regarded with suspicion or disdain by older residents, and was pushed into acquiring the traditional ways of life of the urban middle class. These included investing in property in the town itself and in farmland in the countryside, as well as spending heavily on 'status' goods to compensate for the poor esteem in which the family was held among the town-dwellers. What suffered was the family business, which was left starved of capital. 'Profits are soon diverted to conspicous consumption and social status advancement'.[29]

The last important difference to emerge relates to the families' exposure to and experience of non-agricultural activities, both in old and recent times. Let us consider first of all the way of entry into entrepreneurship in the two areas. As we have shown in this book, in the Comasco there was an initial but failed attempt on the part of peasant-worker families to go into entrepreneurship in traditional artisanal occupations. In the post-war period worker-peasant families became entrepreneurs thanks to the expertise and knowledge acquired by some of their members in the new expanding industries. Many were 'inventors', as we saw: thus they formed their own firm initially to exploit new ideas related to production technology or product specification. They took pride in what they did and collectively contributed to improving the efficiency of the industry in which they operated. The presence of older, leading firms in the area also contributed to the general well-being of the industry. They could be counted on to promote research and development, stimulating other local firms to imitate their processes and products. In short, the presence of under-capitalised, less efficient firms – which also no doubt existed – was more than offset by the activities of the numerous innovators.

In the Marches area studied by Blim peasant–worker families moved directly into entrepreneurship or did so following a short period of apprenticeship in a local factory or workshop, just as they did in Northern Lombardy in the 1920s and 1930s, with the crucial difference that this transition in the Marches was largely successful, thanks to an international mass demand for artisanal-made quality consumer goods such as shoes which was lacking in the 1930s. Economic success, however, may prove short-termed, precisely because a direct transition peasants-workers-entrepreneurs is based almost exclusively on the self-exploitation of the family and only minimally on inventiveness, understanding of the production process and the technologies available, and knowledge of the markets.

The last crucial difference between the two areas concerns their past economic history. The peasant society from which, as Blim shows, present-day entrepreneurs originate, did not engage in diffused rural industries in the nineteenth and early twentieth centuries. The first contacts peasant families had with industrial work came in the post-war period, prior to their moving into entrepreneurship. An important stage of economic and social development which elsewhere led to the acquisition of new skills and a new work discipline appears to be missing. This is an aspect which Blim underrates, with the result that he generalises his findings to the whole of the Marches region and indeed the Third Italy. Yet other studies have shown that the Marches – let alone the Third Italy – do possess areas of diffused industrialisation of the 'advanced' type. It is no coincidence, in our view, that these areas correspond to those affected, in the nineteenth century, by older forms of industrialisation, namely diffused textile domestic industries and factory-based silk manufacturing.[30] Conversely, the Marches town studied by Blim is situated in the economically weaker half of the region, an area largely bypassed by the earlier 'wave' of textile, and particularly silk, manufacturing. Blim does refer to a 'proto-industrial' phase of the shoemaking industry in his book, but he makes it clear that it was restricted to the urban core and did not involve peasant labour.[31] Again, it is probably not a coincidence that when this industry started to affect the countryside, it did so by attracting peasant labour to the towns, not by reaching out into the rural areas.[32]

Figure 6.2 will help clarify the two main paths to diffused entrepreneurship outlined above.

Figure 6.2 Family Paths to Entrepreneurship: Social Factors and Economic Characteristics

PATH 1 (weakly competitive)

Social Factors	**Economic Characteristics**
Peasant–worker family Self-exploitation	
Brief/minimal acquisition of industrial/technical skills	Old/mature technologies Unskilled/semi-skilled labour *lavoro nero*
Status-seeking (attractiveness of property or land acquisition)	Under-capitalised family business
Move to urban environment	Poor social contacts Poor knowledge of markets Dependence on outside buyers

PATH 2 (strongly competitive)

Worker–peasant family Self-exploitation	
Long-term, slow sedimentation of industrial/technical skills	Innovation Technological changes Skilled labour
'Firm' replaces 'farm'	Highly capitalised family business
Rural–urban environment replaces countryside— family stays put	Good social contacts Knowledge of markets Locally-based sales agents/co-ordinators

To sum up, a socially-led drive towards small-scale entrepreneurship, based on a social form which outlived the overcoming of agriculture by industry, appears to have been a common feature of Italy's industrialisation since the start of this century. The ways this entrepreneurial 'propensity' was actually achieved differed from area to area, depending on the various possible – but historically determined – combinations of families, economic activities and territorial settlements. For these reasons it is impossible to generalise over the inherent strength or weakness of Italian industrialisation, as both Sabel and Blim do, with totally divergent conclusions. Whereas some combinations gave rise to efficient and competitive industrial communities, others led to the formation of more unstable and precarious economies. The fact that Italy's small-scale entrepreneurship has a minimum common denominator – a social form which has resulted from a certain kind of contact between agriculture and industry – should not be confused with a uniformity of results.

Notes

1. A. Marshall, *Industry and Trade*, London, 1920 (1st edn. 1919), p. 230; also *Principles of Economics*, London, 1966 (1st edn. 1917).

2. G. Becattini, 'Dal "settore industriale" al "distretto industriale". Alcune considerazioni sull'unità d'indagine dell'economia industriale', *Rivista di economia e politica industriale*, vol.5, no.1, 1979. Also, 'Il distretto industriale come unità d'indagine', in G. Becattini (ed.), *Mercato e forze locali: il distretto industriale*, Bologna 1987.

3. S. Brusco and C. Sabel, 'Artisan Production and Economic Growth', in F. Wilkinson (ed.), *The Dynamics of Labour Market Segmentation*, London 1981; S. Brusco, 'Productive Decentralisation and Social Integration: The Emilian Model', *Cambridge Journal of Economics*, 6, 1982. Also 'Small Firms and Industrial Districts: the Experience of Italy', in D. Keeble and E. Wever (eds), *New Firms and Regional Development in Europe*, London 1986.

4. G. Garofoli, 'Le aree-sistema in Italia', *Politica ed economia*, vol.11, 1983.

5. For a systematic survey of 'system-areas' in Lombardy see G. Garofoli, *Industrializzazione diffusa in Lombardia*, Milan 1983.

6. G. Becattini, 'Riflessioni sul distretto industriale marshalliano come concetto socio-economico', *Stato e Mercato*, 25, p. 128.

7. Ibid., p. 128.

8. Centro Studi Confindustria, *Evoluzione dei settori industriali*, Rome 1981 to 1990.

9. *La Repubblica*, 24 April 1987.

10. Garofoli, *Industrializzazione diffusa*, pp. 79–80.

11. The information that follows is based on A. Bull's re-elaboration of 1981 census data and draws on the results of the already mentioned research project on Como's small textile firms.

12. A. Bagnasco, *Tre Italie. La problematica territoriale dello sviluppo italiano*, Bologna 1977.

13. M. Paci, *La struttura sociale italiana*, Bologna 1982, pp. 109–24.

14. See M. Forni, *Storie familiari e storie di proprietà* pp. 71–8. Also, M. Barbagli, V. Capecchi and A. Cobalti, *La mobilità sociale in Emilia-Romagna*, Bologna, 1988, pp. 176–89.

15. Brusco, 'Small Firms and Industrial Districts', p. 196.

16. A. Bagnasco, *La costruzione sociale del mercato*, Bologna 1988, p. 123.

17. Brusco, 'Small Firms and Industrial Districts', pp. 196–7.

18. G. Lorenzoni and O. Ornati,'Constellations of firms and new ventures', *Journal of Business Venturing*, 3, 1988.

19. Trigilia, *Grandi partiti e piccole imprese: Communisti e democristiani nelle regioni a economia diffusa*, Bologna 1986.

20. Brusco, 'Small Firms and Industrial Districts', p. 200.

21. R. Y. Nanetti, *Growth and Territorial Policies: The Italian Model of Social Capitalism*, London and New York, 1988, p. 81.

22. Ibid., p. 102.

23. L. Weiss, *Creating Capitalism. The State and Small Business since 1945*, Oxford 1988.

24. P. Hirst and J. Zeitlin (eds), *Reversing Industrial Decline? Industrial Structure and Policy in Britain and her Competitors*, Oxford 1989, p. 2. On flexible specialisation see also M. Piore and C. Sabel, *The Second Industrial Divide: Possibilities for Prosperity*, New York 1984; C. Sabel and J. Zeitlin, 'Historical alternatives to mass production, pp. 133–76.

25. See for example A. Pollert, 'The "flexible firm". Flirtation or Fact?', *Work, Employment and Society*, 2, June 1988, pp. 141–68. Also A. Rannie, *Industrial Relations in Small Firms: Small isn't Beautiful*, London 1989.

26. A. Amin, 'Specialisation without growth: small footwear firms in an inner-city area of Naples', in E. Goodman, J. Bamford and P. Saynor (eds), *Small Firms and Industrial Districts in Europe*, London and New York 1989. Amin argues that the shoe industry in the Neapolitan area known as 'Stella' relies on traditional forms of labour exploitation, and is chronically starved of capital and helplessly short-termist in outlook.

27. M. Blim, *Made in Italy. Small Scale Industrialisation and its Consequences*, New York, Westport and London 1990. The author analyses the post-war industrialisation of a shoemaking town in the Marches region. He traces its origins to the entrepreneurial efforts of

extended families of largely rural stock and argues that the social basis of small-scale industry now acts as a brake to further economic development. Blim rejects the theory that Italy's diffused industrialisation constitutes an advanced model of craft production ('flexible specialisation'), using his case-study to argue instead that its rise was due primarily to particularly favourable international and internal conditions and that its decline has already started.

28. Ibid., pp. 177–215 and 257–64. Also Paci, *La struttura sociale italiana*, p. 123.

29. Ibid., p. 258.

30. C. Zacchia, 'Il quadro economico regionale dal dopoguerra a oggi' in S. Anselmi (ed.), *Storia d'Italia. Le Regioni dall'Unità a oggi. Le Marche*, Turin 1987, pp.407–10, and E. Sori, 'Dala manifattura all'industria', ibid., pp. 326–42.

31. Blim, *Made in Italy*, p. 42.

32. The literature on the Third Italy often refers to the presence of protoindustrial activities, in the nineteenth century and even earlier, in the regions which have recently industrialised. As for northern Italy, Dewerpe has shown that all the sub-Alpine areas affected by protoindustrialisation in the nineteenth century successfully industrialised in the twentieth. Conversely, the absence of earlier forms of rural or diffused industry has been considered one of the reasons for the failure of the province of Ravenna (Emilia-Romagna) to develop any significant community of small firms. See M. Pezzini, 'The small firm economy's odd man out: the case of Ravenna', in E. Goodman *et al.*, *Small Firms and Industrial Districts*. For Dewerpe, see A. Dewerpe, *L'industrie aux champs*.

7
Conclusions

The passage from peasant to entrepreneur took more than a century and involved many generations. Indeed, one of the features of the process is that of the *slow* evolution of the peasant family and of its essential stability, even in the midst of fairly constant economic change. Far from being the protagonists of an agrarian revolution, Lombard peasants showed a remarkable capacity to adapt to changing circumstances while at the same time conserving their established patterns of behaviour and their particular mode of survival. Centred around a piece of land and a house, peasant families rode the successive waves of the rise and fall of the silk industry, economic crisis, war, and reconstruction without losing their particular identity. Their resistance to urbanisation, to proletarianisation, and to the formation of simple nuclear families remained strong far beyond what seemed usual for an industrialising country. This resistance was consolidated from the 1930s onwards by the attempts – initially largely unsuccessful but hugely successful after the Second World War – to set up small businesses while remaining within the context of the multiple pluriactive family.

This evolution, characteristic of upper Lombardy but – as we have seen – in no way limited to that area, prompts certain observations about the role of the peasant–worker family in the overall picture of Italian industrialisation. Perhaps the most surprising feature of the pattern we have traced is precisely that of gradualness – of the slow evolution of the peasant-worker family. Despite profound transformations around it, the social form of the peasant-worker family remains remarkably stable – simply adapting to those changes and participating in them from the family base. The habits of the nineteenth century, when peasants were the victims of rural industry, are adjusted to the twentieth century, when families of peasant origin become the protagonists of a different kind of diffused industrialisation.

This slow and gradual development in the direction of entrepreneurship would seem to be at odds with that vision of

Italian industrialisation which sees Italy as a 'late comer', compelled to industrialise by forced marches and accelerated change. Romeo's insistence on the necessity for the compression of consumption after Unification in the interests of primitive accumulation is suggestive of a violent process of transition.[1] Equally Gerschenkron's emphasis on the State-backed 'big spurt' necessary for take-off in 'second comer' countries is, in a sense, just as dramatic.[2] It would seem that, in the absence of the myriad of small industrialists who had characterised the English industrial revolution, the State was the only force capable of organising the basic elements of a process of rapid industrialisation.

The example of the Comasco and the Alto Milanese provides a rather different picture. What is striking in these areas is the substantial continuity between economic phases and the absence of radical and rapid transformations. With the possible exception of the First World War, which in any case served to change mentalities rather than structures and to accelerate pre-existing tendencies, the characteristics of the population would seem to be *resistance* to dramatic changes but *acceptance* of gradual adjustments and adaptations. Indeed, survival was based on this continual process of adaptation to opportunities offered. In these areas, therefore, industrialisation was not realised through 'big spurts', but through a slow development of entrepreneurial skills across the varied fortunes of diffused rural industries. The protagonists of this process – the peasant-worker families of the region – managed to combine traditional and novel impulses in such a way as to avoid precisely the kind of dramatic breach which is suggested by the model of accelerated 'second comer' industrialisation, with its implications of rapid proletarianisation and urbanisation for those involved in industrial production.

This is not to underestimate the importance of heavy industry, nor indeed to deny the importance of the role of the State in the formation of that industry. But it is to suggest that – contrary to much of what one reads – a part of Italian industry developed from the outset on lines very different from that of big industry, without creating large towns and an industrial proletariat, and without the intervention of the State. True, the silk industry disappeared in great part, but it left behind it a society predisposed to other initiatives in manufacturing or in commerce. The source of the pluriactive habit might disappear, but the habit itself continued. And this was largely independent of either large industry (which at most might serve as a school of industrial skills to be exploited later on an individual basis) or of the State. In terms of social organisation in relation to industry, the picture which emerges from Como, therefore, is one of considerable continuity over the years, of a prolonged period in which the traditional and the new co-exist, rather than of a traumatic transition from agriculture to industry. Indeed, there is almost a paradoxical conservatism – *the disposition to adapt to anything rather than accept the fundamental and final change represented by the break-up of the family*. Here we have argued that it is precisely this disposition, containing both static and dynamic elements, which preserved the economic unit of the family and generated the spirit of entrepreneurship.

How far does this kind of industrialisation – without separation from the land, without industrial concentration – square with the classic models of industrialisation? Traditional (1950s and 1960s) theories of modernisation, in fact, tended to equate *rural* with farming, agricultural workers, paternalism, primary (kinship) ties and a local, village-based identity. By contrast, they equated *urban* with industry, proletarian workers, political pluralism and secondary ties. The transition from a pre-modern (non-industrial) to a modern (industrial) society was thus seen as the transition from a rural to an urban society. Silk offers us a somewhat different picture, which it may be useful to summarise as follows:

(i) The transition from a cottage industry to the factory system and the resulting mechanisation of production were achieved at a relatively early stage (middle-nineteenth century), but the more these processes were realised, the more they allowed rural–industrial families to remain attached to the land – which, indeed, was one of the purposes of mechanising silk-production. Traditional skilled artisans in the towns were increasingly replaced with unskilled labour in the countryside.

(ii) Population increased at a fast rate but urbanisation remained fairly limited (with the exception of Milan). In the province of Como in 1901 the percentage of people working in industry was on a par with that employed in agriculture, yet the percentage of people living in towns with more than 20,000 inhabitants was only 9 per cent.

(iii) Social modernisation, i.e. the formation of an industrial proletariat, was also fairly limited. A hybrid peasant-worker or worker-peasant class was created in its place.

(iv) Cultural modernisation, for example the replacement of kinship/personalistic ties with collective, impersonal organisations and of a 'resistance to change' attitude with one of 'acceptance of change' by and large did not affect the 'hybrid' workforce and entrepreneurial class created by silk. Families where the man went out to work in the factory constituted a partial exception to this, though in their case collective organisations and an 'acceptance of change' mentality coexisted with rather than replaced primary relationships and traditional attitudes. Localistic, community-based allegiances were only partially broken down to allow for integration into the national society (hence the subcultures, as Trigilia has shown).

Several general points emerge from this analysis. The first is that the apparent anomalies of the Como case should not tempt the simplistic conclusion – often applied to textiles – that we are merely dealing with a case of relative industrial backwardness. The diffused, rural, structure of the silk industry might suggest this, but it would be a conclusion very wide of the mark. Silk created capital on a vast scale, established contacts with most of European markets, generated financial circuits, encouraged entrepreneurship, and formed a disciplined and relatively skilled workforce accustomed to find employment in both agricultural and industrial sectors. Despite its diffused structure, silk was anything but a backward industry. It should not be seen, therefore, simply as a transitional stage towards something more 'modern'. It is here, in fact, that we part company with protoindustrial theory, which tends to consider rural industry as a transitional phase leading to modernisation proper, with its typical sociocultural features, i.e. urbanisation, the formation of an industrial proletariat, the emergence of the 'male breadwinner norm', collective bargaining, a secularised culture, etc. In the case of Italy this aspect of the theory has clearly shown its shortcomings. When applied to the whole large strip of the sub-Alpine hills, the protoindustrial model has failed to take into account the emergence of areas of diffused, small-scale industrialisation, as opposed to areas of mass production in large plants. In this context those characteristics of silk production which appear 'anomalous' in respect of traditional patterns of industrialisation have not been valued for their real significance, but have usually been either ignored or judged to be transitory.

The fact is that the Comasco witnessed transitions of a totally different kind. For the silk-producing areas did not grow into a fully industrial society characterised by urbanisation, a proletarian workforce and large-scale industry. This 'classic' industrialisation took place in other areas, mainly limited to the industrial triangle of Turin, Genoa and Milan, excluding the sub-Alpine countryside. In the silk-producing areas, as we saw in the course of this book, there was no real change in the economic and social structure until after the Second World War; more important, when the second 'wave' of industrialisation finally took place, it still did not possess those features usually associated with full-scale industrial development.

The impact of the early, textile-related industrialisation upon the later development must therefore be viewed from a different angle. That impact was first felt in the later years of the fascist period and produced its own offspring – small-scale industrialisation – in the late thirties, but more particularly from 1945 onwards. Thus an apparently 'anomalous' early industrialisation led to an 'anomalous' mature industrialisation without recreating or imitating the typical features of the urban-based industrial 'big spurt' of the late nineteenth – early twentieth centuries. The picture that emerges, therefore, is that of the contemporaneous development/emergence in temporal succession during the course of the nineteenth century of two different patterns of industrialisation which subsequently proceeded in parallel up to the fascist period. At that point the rurally-based silk industry plunged into deep crisis, but the rural-industrial society it had created re-emerged phoenix-like from its ashes as an industrial-rural world.

It is perhaps worth recalling the essential features of this second wave of industrialisation in rural areas:

(i) Re-industrialisation took place on a diffused basis, affecting the entire countryside. Neighbouring villages formed clusters of industrial specialisms or 'industrial districts'. The majority of the population, as we saw in Chapter 5, were able to continue to live and work in their home villages, gradually adjusting their way of life and cultural values to the changed economy.

(ii) Urbanisation remained fairly limited. In 1951 still only a quarter of the total population of the province of Como lived in towns with more than 20,000 inhabitants. By 1981 the percentage had if anything slightly decreased (23 per cent).

(iii) Social modernisation has been at least partially achieved, since the number of people engaged in agriculture was negligible by 1981 and industrial manual workers accounted for the single largest group of economically active people. Nevertheless, as we showed in Chapters 3 and 4, most families still possessed a plot of land (even if only a vegetable plot) and many industrial workers belonged to pluriactive families with a self-employed head. There was still no clear-cut demarcation between economic occupation and social status.

(iv) Cultural modernisation has also been achieved to a certain extent, as far as full acceptance of the benefits of a free market economy, social mobility and entrepreneurship are concerned. Primary (family) ties, however, continue to play an important role. Political culture has remained stubbornly localistic and community-based, choosing to distance itself from – and indeed to define itself in antithesis to – the central State and the national identity.

Certainly, when compared with 'classic' patterns of industrialisation, this pattern appears to be anomalous. But – from the beginning of this book – we have preferred the term 'specific', precisely because we are unhappy with the idea of normal and abnormal roads to industrialisation. Such an idea inevitably ends by distorting valuations and detracts from what is novel, from the originality of what fails to correspond. In fact, the silk industry represented a specific pattern of industrialisation which took advantage of a relatively unmodernised agricultural system based on the family farm and created in the course of time a specific social form. It was replaced by another (again specific) version of industrialisation based on the same social form and on an original solution to the urban-rural dichotomy.

Since the early (silk-related) and the late (engineering-led) 'waves' of industrialisation together span more than 150 years, it is highly doubtful that they represent a transitional stage which will eventually evolve into the 'classic' model of development. We have to conclude that they represent two variants of a specific model of industrialisation/modernisation characterised by:

(i) A rural–urban environment ('urbanised countryside').

(ii) a social form (the pluriactive family and by extension the local community) which is organic to economic development, as opposed to being a residual feature organic to a pre-modern society which refuses to die out.

(iii) Limited secularisation, which is the outcome of an 'acceptance of change' mentality in the economic sphere, combined with a 'resistance to change' attitude in the socio-political sphere (due to (ii) above rather than to the cultural heritage of a pre-modern society).

To equate the industrial development of the sub-Alpine areas and indeed of the Third Italy with a model of industrialisation in its own right does not mean that it may not eventually grow into a qualitatively different economic and social structure, in the way that societies succeed each other in the historical process. The same, however, may happen to the 'advanced' industrial model of Anglo-Saxon origins, as Sabel and Piore implied when they argued recently that the economic-historical phase characterised by mass production, large industry and the use of unskilled labour (the 'Fordist' phase) is coming to an end.[3] Whether or not this phase will actually be replaced by the 'flexible specialisation' phase, as they envisage, i.e. by a phase which will bear the inprint of the pattern of industrialisation typical of the Third Italy, is another matter. It is not our intention to make predictions for the future, but to try to analyse and to explain the past. Nevertheless, it is significant that their hypothesis reverses the classic interpretations of economic development, judging diffused industrialisation to be the more resilient and durable form and 'Fordism' the transitory stage.

In reality, of course, neither form of industrialisation exists in a vacuum. It would seem more reasonable, in fact, to argue that, in many cases, it is the complementary nature of the relationship between large and small which produces successful industrialisation. It is no coincidence that in Italy the indigenous 'industrial–rural' and the imported 'urban' models of industrialisation have coexisted with each other for more than a century. It is true, though, that their relationship in the past was only an 'indirect' one. Thus the silk industry provided much of the capital used in the expansion of Milan as an economic and commercial centre, contributed massively to the balance of payments, and helped finance the emergence of a capital-goods manufacturing sector. In turn, the formation of the industrial triangle provided pluriactive families of the sub-Alpine areas with an opportunity to widen considerably their extra-farming sources of income and to gain valuable expertise and skills in industrial processes and technologies. It is only recently that the two patterns of industrialisation have started to come together in a 'direct' way, with the move towards de-integration and structural subcontracting on the part of the large firms in the 1970s and 1980s. This was a move which could not have been achieved – or even contemplated – had the industrial-rural, family-based pattern of industrialisation not existed to provide the perfect solution for problems which large industry was experiencing relating to the mass production process and the rigidity of the labour market.

A similar trend has been detected outside Italy, with the increasing relocation of industries in depressed rural areas and the use of 'pluriactive' farming families. This phenomenon is viewed in deeply contrasting ways by observers. Whereas Piore and Sabel have welcomed the move as an example of the search for flexible specialisation, many see the resurgence of the 'informal' economy as a negative and divisive aspect of the restructuring of global capitalism. The role of small firms and family workshops is judged to be subservient to that of the large corporations, and rural areas are seen as subordinated to urban ones.

We discussed these issues in Chapter 5, in relation to the Third Italy. There is little doubt that small-scale industrialisation in rural or semi-rural areas can be either simply a component of the industrial reorganisation of large industry or a successful and independent industrial organisation in its own right. In Italy both types of small-scale industry, which we defined respectively as the weakly competitive and the strongly competitive type, can be detected. In the first case small firms do indeed play a marginal role in respect of the large corporations and global competition. In the second case they are major actors on the international scene.

The existing body of literature on the informal economy, industrial districts, the Third Italy and flexible specialisation has not yet addressed the fundamental question of whether the 'exploitative' and the 'innovative' versions of small-scale localised industry represent two stages of development – so that we can postulate a progressive evolution from the one to the other – or two distinct patterns of industrialisation. Having partially addressed this question for the Italian case and in the historical context, we would be inclined to conclude that there is an element of evolution at work, in the sense that the weak version of localised small business is more commonly found in areas which have only recently experienced their first 'wave' of industrialisation. The opposite tends to be true in the case of the strongly competitive industrial districts.

We also found, however, that, although both types of small-scale industry have similar social origins, they appear to have followed different paths of development. It is here that the existence of an early 'indirect' relationship between rural industry and the 'urban' pattern of industrialisation takes on a new significance. As we argued in Chapter 5, a strongly competitive industrial district correlates well with the presence of earlier forms of rural industry, the acquisition of skills and know-how in large, often urban-based, firms within commuting distance, and the disappearance of full-time farming as an alternative to industrial work or as a lever to achieve upward social mobility. By contrast, in some parts of the Third Italy characterised by weakly competitive businesses, there were virtually no early forms of export-led rural industry and the scope for learning new skills or 'appropriating' the latest technology from large firms was minimal or at best intermittent, given the distance and relative isolation of these businesses from the urban areas of intense industrialisation. Also, full-time farming and/or consumption remained attractive alternatives to industrial entrepreneurship; indeed, the latter may be considered simply instrumental in achieving one of the former.

In conclusion, it may be wise to sound a note of caution. The kind of industrialisation described here, apparently without great shocks and traumas, might seem to be the recipe for success for areas or countries looking for a path towards relatively painless industrial development. Looked at superficially, the pattern of evolution experienced by the Comasco might appear very attractive; in the same way, the Third Italy could seem a model for parts of the 'Third World'. Things would appear fairly simple. Peasant families produce a staple crop; in the process of transforming that crop for export, they learn industrial skills and entrepreneurial habits; they then pass to independent, small-scale, rurally-based, industrial production, at the same time avoiding all the social problems of urbanisation and proletarianisation. It seems too good to be true – and indeed it is. As will be evident from the analysis of the preceding chapters, at each stage of this process a large number of variables operate to determine the passage to – and the successful realisation of – the following stage. In the Italian case, as we have tried to make clear, the historical background is extremely important. The north of Italy, as part of the Austro-Hungarian Empire, was subject to the economic stimuli of the changes in the rest of Europe from the middle of the eighteenth century, and this was reflected in development in both agriculture and manufacturing. Silk did not appear from nowhere. At the same time, it is useful to remember that silk was itself a rather unique crop, necessarily involving the rural population in both agricultural and industrial production at a certain level of technical sophistication. The same cannot be said of many other staple crops.

Yet the product is not the whole story; as is obvious, many export-directed staples have failed to produce industrialisation. Also fundamental is the relationship of the peasants with the land. In this respect, it is necessary to go no further than Southern Italy to understand the difficulties of translating the 'rural-industrial' model to other areas. An agricultural structure completely different from the north, with a wholly different relationship between peasants and the land, prevented the establishment of the multiple family on the northern model, centred on a house and a plot of land. Because of this, families remained totally dependent on the land and were never able to expand into non-agricultural activities – where these existed – with any degree of success. And even when and where this was possible, the products involved conveyed few skills. In this sense, it has to be recognised that the preparation of agricultural products for export – canning tomatoes, bottling oil and wine, packing fruit – is not the same, from the point of view of training a workforce, as spinning and weaving silk. As a consequence, the pluriactive family – with its entrepreneurial tendencies – never developed in the same way. The dualism apparent in Italian development originates in part from here – from a social and agrarian structure, established long before Unification, which was incapable of expressing the same kind of transformation as that of the north.

This is just another way of saying that there is no magic formula leading to industrialisation based on small businesses. The variables we have mentioned here – the type of staple product, the nature of the demand, the social relations in agriculture, the technological content of transformation – are only a few of the factors which condition development. All we have attempted to do in this study is to establish certain of the historical origins of this kind of industrialisation and to assess its likely viability. We suggest that small-scale business industrialisation is neither anomalous nor transitory, but conforms to a logic which is fully understandable in historical terms. On the other hand, the diversity of performance of present-day small business continues to give rise to debate and has not yet been analysed or explained conclusively. Some areas of small-firm development have been particularly successful in acquiring a strategic position in the world economy, while others are struggling and experiencing industrial decline. This diversity will no doubt serve to encourage further studies of the growing history of rurally-based industrialisation – studies which will certainly become richer as the perspective grows ever longer.

Notes

1. R. Romeo, *Risorgimento e capitalismo*, Bari 1959.

2. A. Gerschenkron, *Economic Backwardness in Historical Perspective*, Cambridge 1962.

3. Piore and Sabel, *The Second Industrial Divide*.

Bibliography

Allum, P. and Diamanti, I., '50/'80,vent'anni. *Due generazioni di giovani a confronto*, Roma 1986

Amin, A., 'Specialisation without growth: small footwear firms in an inner-city area of Naples', in E. Goodman, J. Bamford and P. Saynor (eds), *Small Firms and Industrial Districts in Europe*, London and New York 1989

Angeli, S., *Proprietari, commercianti e filandieri a Milano nel primo ottocento*, Milan 1982

Annuario statistico della emigrazione italiana dal 1876 al 1925 con notizie sulla emigrazione negli anni 1869 –875, Rome 1926

Atti della Commissione Parlamentare d'Inchiesta sulla disoccupazione, Vol.III, Tomo 1, Camera dei Deputati, Rome, 1953

Atti della Giunta Parlamentare per l'Inchiesta agraria e sulle condizioni della classe agricola, Rome 1884, vol.VI, fasc.2, Monografia del circondario di Como; Monografia del circondario di Lecco; Relazione finale

Avogadro, A., *La Pia Azienda Tessile. I provvedimenti per gli operai disoccupati a Como*, Como 1891.

Bagnasco, A., *La costruzione sociale del mercato*, Bologna 1988

Bagnasco, A., *Tre Italie. La problematica territoriale dello sviluppo italiano*, Bologna 1977

Ballestrero M. V., and Levrero, R., *Genocidio perfetto. Industrializzazione e forza-lavoro nel Lecchese 1840–1870*, Milan 1979.

Barbagli, M., Capecchi, V. and Cobalti, A., *La mobilità sociale in Emilia–Romagna*, Bologna, 1988

Barbagli, M., *Sotto lo stesso tetto. Mutamenti della famiglia in Italia dal XV al XX secolo*, Bologna 1984

Bari, A., *Sull'avvenire degli Operai Tessitori della Fabbricazione di Como*, Como 1890

Becattini, G., 'Dal "settore industriale" al "distretto industriale". Alcune considerazioni sull'unità d'indagine dell'economia industriale', in *Rivista di economia e politica industriale*, 5, 1, 1979.

Becattini, G., 'Il distretto industriale come unità d'indagine', in id.(ed.), *Mercato e forze locali: il distretto industriale*, Bologna 1987

Becattini, G., 'Riflessioni sul distretto industriale marshalliano come concetto socio-economico', *Stato e Mercato*, 25

Becattini, G., 'Riflessioni sullo sviluppo socio-economico della

Toscana', in *Storia d'Italia, Le regioni dall'Unità ad oggi: la Toscana* (ed. G. Mori), Turin 1986

Beldam, C., *Raw Silk: a peasant industry in the Brianza*, London 1898

Blim, M., *Made in Italy. Small Scale Industrialisation and its Consequences*, New York, Westport and London 1990

Bonomelli, G., *Tre mesi al di là delle Alpi*, Milan– Sesto S. Giovanni, 1914.

Bonomi, S., 'Intorno alle condizioni igieniche degli operai e in particolare delle operaje in seta nella provincia di Como', in *Annali Universali di Medicina*, 225, 1873

Brunetta, E., 'Dalla Grande Guerra alla Repubblica', in *Storia d'Italia. Le Regioni dall'Unita a oggi. Il Veneto* (ed. S.Lanaro), Turin, 1984

Brusco, S. and Sabel, C., 'Artisan Production and Economic Growth', in F. Wilkinson (ed.), *The Dynamics of Labour Market Segmentation*, London, 1981.

Brusco, S., 'Productive Decentralisation and Social Integration: The Emilian Model', *Cambridge Journal of Economics*, 6, 1982

Brusco, S., 'Small Firms and Industrial Districts in Italy', in D. Keeble and E. Wever (eds), *New Firms and Regional Development in Europe*, London, 1986

Brusco, S., *Agricoltura ricca e classi sociali*, Milan 1979

Cafagna, L., 'La 'rivoluzione agraria'in Lombardia', in *Annali dell'Istituto Giangiacomo Feltrinelli*, vol. II, 1959

Cafagna,L., *Dualismo e sviluppo nella storia d'Italia*, Venice 1989.

Canetta, R., 'Aspetti di vita religiosa e sociale nel Basso Comasco alla fine dell'Ottocento', in *Bollettino dell'Archivio per la storia del Movimento sociale cattolico in Italia*, XI, 1976

Cento Bull, A., 'Protoindustrialization, small-scale capital accumulation and diffused entrepreneurship. The case of the Brianza in Lombardy (1860–1950)', *Social History*, 14, 2, 1989

Cento Bull, A., 'The Lombard silk workers in the nineteenth century: an industrial workforce in a rural setting', in *The Italianist*, 7, 1987

Cento Bull, A.,'Appunti per un'analisi della famiglia operaia e contadina sotto il fascismo', *Studi e Ricerche di Storia Contemporanea*, no.16, Bergamo, 1981

Cento Bull A., 'La *Lega Lombarda*. A new political subculture for Lombardy's localised industries', in *The Italinist*, Vol. 12, 1992.

Consonni, G. and Tonon, G., 'Casa e lavoro nell'area milanese: dalla fine dell'ottocento all'avvento del fascismo' in *Classe* 14, 1977

Corner, P., *Fascism in Ferrara 1915–25*, Oxford 1975

Corner, P., 'Fascist agrarian policy and the Italian economy in the inter-war years', in J. A. Davis (ed.), *Gramsci and Italy's Passive Revolution*, London 1979

Corner, P., 'Manodopera agricola e industria manifatturiera nella Lombardia postunitaria' in *Studi storici*, 25, 1984

Corner, P., 'Italy', in S. Salter and J. Stevenson (eds), *The Working Class and Politics in Europe and America 1929–45*, London 1989

Corner, P., 'Il contadino – operaio dell'Italia padana' in P. Bevilacqua (ed.), *Storia dell'agricoltura italiana in eta' contemporanea*. II. Uomini e classi, Venezia 1990

Corner, P., *Dall'agricoltura all'industria*, Milan 1992

Corner, P., 'Women and fascism. Changing family roles in the transition from an agricultural to an industrial society' in *European History Quarterly*, 23, 1, 1993.

Cristofoli M. and Pozzobon M., *I tessili milanesi. Le fabbriche, gli industriali, i lavoratori, il sindacato dall'Ottocento agli anni '30*, Milan 1981

Davis, J.A., *Conflict and Control. Law and Order in Nineteenth Century Italy*, London 1988

De Clementi, A., 'Appunti sulla formazione della classe operaia in Italia', in *Studi storici*, 32, 1976

De Maddalena, A., 'Rilievi sull'esperienza demografica ed economica milanese dal 1861 al 1915', in (various authors), *L'economia italiana dal 1861 al 1961*, Milan 1961

Del Re, A., 'I patti agrari dell'Alto Milanese dalla restaurazione contrattuale fascista alla grande crisi', in (various authors), *Agricoltura e forze sociali in Lombardia nella crisi degli anni trenta*, Milan 1983

Della Peruta, F., *Democrazia e socialismo nel Risorgimento*, Rome 1973.

Della Peruta, F.,Leydi, R. and Stella, A., *Mondo popolare in Lombardia. Milano e il suo territorio*, Milan, 1985

Dewerpe, A., *L'industrie aux champs. Essai sur la proto-industrialisation en Italie du Nord (1800–1880)*, Rome 1985.

Errera, A., 'Inchiesta sulle condizioni degli operai nelle fabbriche', in Archivio di statistica 1879

Forni, M., *Storie familiari e storie di proprietà*, Turin 1987.

Frattini, G., *Storia e statistica delle industrie manufatturiere in Lombardia*, Milan 1856

Garofoli, G., 'Le aree-sistema in Italia', *Politica ed economia*, vol.11, 1983

Garofoli, G., *Industrializzazione diffusa in Lombardia*, Milan 1983

Gerschenkron, A., *Economic Backwardness in Historical Perspective*, Cambridge 1962

Ginsborg, P.,*A History of Contemporary Italy. Society and Politics 1943–1988*, London 1990.

Giorgetti, G., *Contadini e proprietari nell'Italia moderna. Rapporti di produzione e contratti agrari dal secolo XVI a oggi*, Turin 1974

Greenfield, K.R., *Economics and Liberalism in the Risorgimento. A Study of Nationalism in Lombardy 1815–1848*, Baltimore 1934

Griglia, R., (ed.), *La Grande Brianza*, Milan, 1978

Gruner, E., 'Studi sulle condizioni del contadino in Lombardia: abitazioni rurali, condizioni economiche di lavoro, alimentazione', in *Annuario della Istituzione Agraria Dott. A. Ponti*, VI, Milan 1906

Hirst, P. and Zeitlin, J., (eds), *Reversing Industrial Decline? Industrial Structure and Policy in Britain and her Competitors*, Oxford 1989

Hunecke, V., *Classe operaia e rivoluzione industriale a Milano 1859–1892*, Bologna 1982

Istituto Centrale di Statistica, *Sommario di statistiche storiche italiane 1861–1955*, Rome 1958

Istituto Nazionale di Economia Agraria, *La distribuzione della proprietà fondiaria in Italia: Lombardia*, ed. G. Medici, Rome, 1951

Istituto Nazionale di Economia Agraria, *Rapporti fra proprietà, impresa e mano d'opera nell' agricoltura italiana, XIV, Lombardia* (relatore G. Medici), Rome 1932

Jacini, S., *La proprietà fondiaria e le popolazioni agricole in Lombardia*, Milan and Verona 1957

Landes, D., (ed.), *A che servono i padroni? Le alternative storiche dell'industrializzazione*, Turin 1987

Lasorsa, G., *L'artigianato in Italia*, Ministero dell'Industria e del Commercio, Direzione Generale dell'Artigianato e delle piccole industrie, Rome, 1963

Lequin, Y., *Les Ouvriers de la région lyonnaise (1848–1914)*, Lyons, 1977

Lorenzoni, G. and Ornati, O., 'Constellations of firms and new ventures', *Journal of Business Venturing*, 3, 1988

Lorenzoni, G., *Inchiesta sulla piccola proprietà coltivatrice formatasi nel dopoguerra. Relazione finale: l'ascesa del contadino italiano nel dopoguerra*, Roma 1938

Luzzatto, G., *L'economia italiana dal 1861 al 1894*, Turin 1968

Manoukian, A., 'La famiglia dei contadini', in P. Melograni (ed.), *La famiglia italiana dall'Ottocento a oggi*, Rome-Bari 1988

Marabini, A., 'Spostamenti di classe nelle campagne italiane', in *Lo Stato Operaio*, 1934, 7

Marshall, A., *Industry and Trade*, London, 1920 (1st edn. 1919)

Marshall, A., *Principles of Economics*, London, 1966 (1st edn. 1917)

Memoria del Comitato Provinciale Comasco della Lega di Difesa Agraria sull'attuale agitazione dei contadini nell'Alto Comasco, Como 1889

Merli, S., *Proletariato di fabbrica e capitalismo industriale. Il caso italiano 1880–1900*, Florence 1972

Merzario, L., *Il capitalismo nelle montagne: strategie famigliari nella prima fase di industrializzazione nel Comasco*, Bologna 1989

Ministero Agricoltura Industria Commercio, *Atti del Comitato dell'Inchiesta industriale*, Rome – Florence 1873–74

Ministero Agricoltura Industria Commercio, *Atti della Commissione d'inchiesta per la industria bacologica e serica*, Rome 1910 – 11

Ministero Agricoltura Industria Commercio, *Bollettino dell'Ufficio del Lavoro*, Rome 1915–1918

Ministero Agricoltura Industria Commercio, *Catasto agrario del regno d'Italia, II, compartimento di Lombardia*, Rome 1913

Molinari, A., *Contratti di lavoro e salari nelle aziende agricole dell'Alto e Basso Milanese*, Milan 1923

Mori, G., 'Materiali,temi ed ipotesi per una storia dell'industria nella regione toscana durante il fascismo (1923–39)', in (various authors), *La Toscana nel regime fascista*, Florence 1971

Nanetti, R. Y., *Growth and Territorial Policies: The Italian Model of Social Capitalism*, London and New York, 1988

Osnaghi Dodi, L., 'Sfruttamento del lavoro nell'industria tessile comasca e prime esperienze di organizzazione operaia', in *Classe*, 5, 1972.

Paci, M., *La struttura sociale italiana*, Bologna 1982

Papa, A., 'Guerra e terra 1915 – 1918', in *Studi storici*, X, 1, 1969

Pescarolo, A. and Ravenni, G. B., *Il proletariato invisibile. La manifattura della paglia nella Toscana mezzadrile (1820–1950)*, Milan 1991.

Pezzini, M., 'The small firm economy's odd man out: the case of Ravenna', in E. Goodman, J. Bamford and P. Saynor (eds), *Small Firms and Industrial Districts in Europe*, London and New York 1989

Piore, M. and Sabel, C., *The Second Industrial Divide: Possibilities for Prosperity*, New York 1984

Pitt, M., Szarka, J. and Bull, A., 'Executive Characteristics, Strategic Choices and Small Firm Development: A Three-Country Study of Small Textile and Clothing Firms', *International Small Business Journal*, vol.9, no.3, April–June 1991

Pollert, A., 'The "flexible firm". Flirtation or Fact?', *Work, Employment and Society*, 2, June 1988

Poni, C., 'All'origine del sistema di fabbrica: tecnologia ed organizzazione produttiva dei mulini di seta nell'Italia settentrionale (sec. XVII–XVIII)', in *Rivista Storica Italiana*, III, 1976

Poni, C., *Fosse e cavedagne benedicon le campagne*, Bologna 1982

Preti, D., 'L'economia toscana nel periodo fascista', in *Storia d'Italia, Le Regioni dall'Unità ad oggi: la Toscana* (ed. G. Mori), Turin 1986

Procacci, Giovanna (ed.), *Stato e classe operaia in Italia durante la prima guerra mondiale*, Milan 1983

Procacci, Giovanna, 'Dalla rassegnazione alla rivolta: osservazioni sul comportamento popolare in Italia negli anni della prima guerra mondiale', in *Ricerche storiche*, XIX, 1, 1989

Procacci, Giuliano, *La lotta di classe in Italia agli inizi del secolo XX*, Rome 1970

Ramella, F., *Terra e telai. Sistemi di parentela e manifattura nel Biellese dell'Ottocento*, Turin 1984

Rannie, A., *Industrial Relations in Small Firms: Small isn't Beautiful*, London, 1989

Romani, M., *L'agricoltura in Lombardia dal periodo delle riforme al 1859*, Milan 1955

Romani, M., *Un secolo di vita agricola in Lombardia (1861–1961)*, Milan 1963

Romeo, R., *Risorgimento e capitalismo*, Bari 1959

Rossi, R., *Inchiesta sulla piccola proprietà coltivatrice formatasi nel dopoguerra*, Lombardia, Rome 1931

Roverato, G., 'La terza regione industriale', in *Storia d'Italia. Le Regioni dall'Unità a oggi. Il Veneto* (ed. S.Lanaro), Turin, 1984

Rusconi, G., *Salviamo una industria gloriosa! I setaioli e la nazione*, Milan 1923.

Sabbatucci-Severino, P. and Trento, A., 'Alcuni cenni sul mercato del lavoro durante il fascismo', in *Quaderni storici*, 29–30, 1975

Sabel, C., and Zeitlin, J., 'Historical alternatives to mass production: politics, markets and technology in nineteenth century industrialisation', *Past and Present*, CVIII, 1985.

Sacchi, G. 'Sullo stato dei fanciulli occupati nelle manifatture', in *Annali universali di statistica*, LXXVIII, 1843

Sapelli, G., (ed.), *La classe operaia durante il fascismo, Annali della Fondazione G. Feltrinelli*, XX, Milan, 1981.

Sereni, E., *Il capitalismo nelle campagne*, Turin 1947.

Serpieri, A., *Il contratto agrario e le condizioni dei contadini nell'Alto Milanese*, Milan 1910

Serpieri, A., *La guerra e le classi rurali italiane*, Bari 1930

Seton-Watson, C., *Italy from Liberalism to Fascism*, London 1969

Sioli Legnani, S., *L'alimentazione del contadino dell'Alto Milanese. Come e' come dovrebbe essere*, Milano 1909

Sori, E., 'Dalla manifattura all'industria' in S. Anselmi (ed.), *Storia d'Italia. Le Regioni dall'Unità a oggi. Le Marche*, Turin 1987

Taverna, L., *I contratti colonici nell'Alto Milanese*, Milan 1909

Tomassini, L.,'Mobilitazione industriale e classe operaia'in Procacci, Giovanna (ed.), *Stato e classe operaia in Italia durante la prima guerra mondiale*, Milan 1983

Trigilia, C., *Grandi partiti e piccole imprese: comunisti e democristiani nelle regioni a economia diffusa*, Bologna 1986.

Ufficio provinciale dell'economia – Como, *Lineamenti e dati dell'attività economica provinciale 1927–1928–1929*, Como 1930

Ufficio provinciale dell'economia – Como, *Alcuni dati statistici sull'economia della provincia*, Como 1929.

Villani, P., 'La storia sociale: problemi e prospettive di ricerca', in *Storia d'Italia Einaudi*, Annali 1, 1979.

Weiss, L., *Creating Capitalism. The State and Small Business since 1945*, Oxford, 1988

Woolf, S. J., *The Poor in Western Europe*, London 1986

Young, A., *Travels during the years 1787,1788, and 1789*, London 1794

Zacchia, C., 'Il quadro economico regionale dal dopoguerra a oggi' in S. Anselmi (ed.), *Storia d'Italia. Le Regioni dall'Unità a oggi. Le Marche*, Turin 1987

Index